Private Collection

Private Collection

recipes from the Junior League of Palo Alto

edited by Bonnie Stewart Mickelson

The Junior League of Palo Alto, Inc.
555 Ravenswood Avenue, Menlo Park
California 94025
© 1980 by The Junior League
of Palo Alto, Inc.
Printed in the United States of America
First Published in September 1980
Second Impression December 1980
Third Impression June 1981

The proceeds from the sale of this book will be returned to the community
through projects sponsored by the Junior League of Palo Alto, Inc.

THE COMMITTEE
1978–1980

Joan Emery Hagey, *Chairman*
Suzanne Lafferty Beim, *Assistant Chairman*
Bonnie Stewart Mickelson, *Editor*

Karen Wyman Bageman   Carolyn Fulgham Butcher
Sarah Mitchell Clark   Letitia Doud Ferrari
Ginger Alfs Glockner   Betty Wassell Hill
Lynn Hochschwender McGowin   Virginia Rockwell Nile
Inge-Lise Nielsen Parker   Dianne Johnson Pitts
Karen Strandhagen Ross   Sonia Wakefield Shepard
Karen Garling Sickel   Christine Larson Terborgh
Catharine Howell Zander

Nancy Sothern Mueller, *Chairman, 1980-1981*
Patricia Ireland Fuller, *Chairman, 1980-1981*

Bonnie Stewart Mickelson, *Co-chairman, 1976-1977*
Sonia Wakefield Shepard, *Co-chairman, 1976-1977*

Margaret Snyder Hinman, *Chairman, 1975-1976*

Virginia Vlack Tedrow, *Chairman, 1974-1975*

Our singular purpose in producing this cookbook has been to provide the most loved and consistently successful recipes for entertaining from those submitted by members of our Junior League who are recognized as accomplished cooks and hostesses. Most of these recipes have been treasured by their donors for many years, sometimes generations. We have tested each dish numerable times, and have tried to present all instructions as completely but simply as possible, so that novice and expert cooks, alike, are satisfied. May these recipes bring you as much pleasure as they have us.

The Committee

*To Aunt Bea and Aunt Jane...
to each mother, grandmother, and dear friend
who has taught, inspired, and encouraged us,
and has given so generously of her own
"private collection".*

AVOCADO and MUSHROOM PIQUANT

pi·quant \ˈpē·kənt \ adj. 1.: pleasantly savory 2.: having a lively charm . . . a tasty first course.

Serves 8

*Preparation
20 minutes*

*Marinate
3 hours*

2 avocados
½ pound small mushrooms
½ cup oil
3 tablespoons tarragon vinegar
2 tablespoons lemon juice
2 tablespoons water
1 tablespoon chopped parsley
1 clove garlic, minced
¾ teaspoon salt
Freshly ground pepper

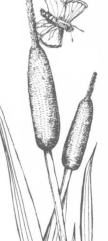

Peel and slice avocados. Remove stems from mushrooms. Peel caps, if necessary.

Blend remaining ingredients and pour over avocado slices and mushroom caps. Chill several hours, spooning the dressing over the vegetables several times.

Serve on attractive lettuce leaves on small plates with sprigs of watercress or parsley.

This recipe is also nice as a garnish with steak or salmon.

2 SCALLOPS in WATERCRESS

Serves
6–8

Preparation
20 minutes

The fresh and vibrant color of the sauce combined with the delicate texture of the scallops makes this a most inviting, as well as delicious, first course.

½ cup dry vermouth
½ onion, sliced
Sprig of parsley
1 bay leaf
Salt and pepper to taste
1 pound sea scallops, cut in bite-sized pieces

In a large saucepan, heat the vermouth, onion, parsley, bay leaf, and salt and pepper. Add the scallops and simmer gently until just cooked through, about 5–7 minutes, occasionally stirring carefully with a wooden spoon. Do not overcook.

Remove the scallops to a separate bowl, reserving the broth with the onion and parsley for soups or stocks.

WATERCRESS SAUCE

1 cup mayonnaise
½ cup chopped watercress
¼ cup chopped parsley
¼ cup chopped chives or scallions
1½ teaspoons chopped fresh dill (or ½ teaspoon dried)
2 teaspoons lime juice

In an electric blender, combine all sauce ingredients and blend until smooth. Chill the scallops and sauce separately until ready to serve.

For individual servings, place pretty leaves of butter or Bibb lettuce on scallop shells or small plates. Divide the scallops among them and top with the sauce. For a buffet, line a glass bowl with lettuce leaves, fill with the scallops and dress with the sauce. Use sprigs of watercress and chopped parsley for garnishes.

ROSEMARY WALNUTS 3

These make a wonderful "hostess gift", and they are irresistible with cocktails.

Yield
4 cups

6 tablespoons butter
1 tablespoon dried rosemary, crumbled
1 tablespoon salt
½ teaspoon cayenne pepper
4 cups walnut halves

Preparation
5 minutes

Baking
15 minutes

Melt butter in a large sauce pan. Remove from heat and add seasonings. Add the walnuts and toss gently but well. Place the walnuts in a shallow roasting pan in one layer. Bake at 325° until richly brown, about 10–15 minutes, shaking occasionally. They are nicest served warm.

CAVIAR PIE 4

One may fear to try this since caviar has a limited number of enthusiasts, but our committee and respective husbands gave this recipe unanimous raves. Although an elegant dish, you may use inexpensive caviar. Serve as a first course on dainty glass plates with sprigs of watercress and thin lemon slices, or in tartlet form for a midnight supper with champagne.

Serves 12

Preparation
10 minutes

Draining
overnight

1 pint sour cream
Juice of 1 small lemon
1 9-inch baked pastry shell
2 tablespoons minced chives
8 ounces caviar

Place sour cream in a cheese cloth or clean kitchen towel and hang over a bowl for several hours or overnight to drain.

Add lemon juice to sour cream and blend well. Spread mixture into pastry shell. Sprinkle with chives and gently spread caviar over top. Cover with plastic wrap and refrigerate for several hours, then cut the pie into wedges to serve.

5 COUNTRY TERRINE

Serves
25 plus

Preparation
1 ½ hours

Baking
1 ½ hours

A large, very handsome pâté, with the pistachios adding special character. Feature it on a holiday buffet or for a glamorous picnic in the country with French bread and cornichons and that favorite bottle of wine.

¾ pound bacon
1 tablespoon butter
1 onion, chopped
1 pound pork (½ fat, ½ lean), ground
½ pound veal, finely chopped
½ pound chicken livers, finely chopped
½ cup shelled pistachios
2 cloves garlic, crushed
¼ teaspoon ground allspice
Pinch of ground cloves
Pinch of ground nutmeg
2 small eggs, lightly beaten
½ cup heavy cream
2 tablespoons brandy
Salt and pepper
½ pound ham, cut in thin strips
1 bay leaf

Preheat oven to 350°.

Use a 2-quart terrine with a tight lid. Line the terrine with the bacon, reserving a few slices for the top.

Melt the butter in a small pan and sauté the onion until soft but not brown. Combine with remaining ingredients except the ham strips and bay leaf. Check seasoning. It should have a generous amount of salt and pepper.

Spread ⅓ of the mixture in the terrine. Layer with half of the ham strips and repeat. Cover with last third of meat mixture. Lay remaining slices of bacon on top and then the bay leaf. Place the lid on top of the terrine and seal it with a luting paste made of ⅓ cup flour and ⅔ tablespoons water.

Set the terrine in a shallow roasting pan filled with 2–3 inches hot water. Bake 1½ hours.

Cool terrine until it is tepid before removing luting paste and lid. Then press the pâté, still in its terrine, with 2 pounds of weight (canned goods work well as weights) until cold. Refrigerate 3 days before serving or up to a week.

As a first course, slice and serve on butter lettuce with cornichons and thin slices of French bread.

6 GAZPACHO

The best we've had.

Preparation
20 minutes

Chill
2 hours

1 large tomato, peeled and seeded
½ small onion
½ cucumber
½ green pepper
1 large celery stalk
2 teaspoons finely chopped parsley
1 teaspoon finely chopped chives
1 small clove garlic, minced
2 cups tomato-vegetable juice
2–3 tablespoons red wine vinegar
2 tablespoons olive oil
1 tablespoon lemon juice
1 teaspoon sugar
1 teaspoon salt
¼ teaspoon white pepper
½ teaspoon Worcestershire sauce
⅛ teaspoon Tabasco sauce

Finely chop all vegetables. (A food processor is ideal for this.) Combine with remaining ingredients and refrigerate until very cold.

Serve in chilled bowls and pass an assortment of garnishes such as *chopped hard-cooked egg whites, sieved hard-cooked egg yolks, finely chopped green onions* or more *chives, croutons, bacon bits*, and *chopped avocado.*

We serve this hot or cold, garnished with thin slices of lemon and a sprinkling of minced parsley. The handwork adds a little extra time, but it's worth it.

Serves 8

Preparation 30 minutes

Cooking 1 ¼ hours

   4 large artichokes (or 6 medium)
   1 bay leaf
   2 tablespoons lemon juice

Cover artichokes with salted water, adding bay leaf and lemon juice. Simmer until artichokes are tender, about 45 minutes to 1 hour. Drain and cool. Remove chokes and scrape the meat from leaves. Chop hearts.

   ½ cup finely chopped onion
   ½ cup finely chopped celery
   6 tablespoons butter
   6 tablespoons flour
   6 cups chicken broth
   ¼ cup lemon juice
   1 bay leaf
   1 teaspoon salt
   ¼ teaspoon white pepper
   ¼ teaspoon thyme
   ¼ teaspoon grated nutmeg (optional)
   1¾ cups milk
   ¼ cup sour cream
   2 egg yolks, beaten

Sauté onion and celery in butter until soft. Add flour. Cook 1 minute, stirring constantly, then blend in broth and lemon juice. Add bay leaf, salt, pepper, thyme, nutmeg, artichoke scrapings and hearts. Cover and simmer 20 minutes. Puree in a blender.

Mix together milk, sour cream, and egg yolks. If serving the soup cold, stir in milk mixture with a whisk, correct seasonings and chill. If serving hot, heat the soup to boiling point, remove from heat, and briskly add milk mixture with a whisk. Correct seasonings and keep heated over hot water.

8 ENGLISH CUCUMBER SOUP

Yield
8 cups

Preparation
15 minutes

Perfect for that hot, hot day, there are a variety of ways it may be served . . . as the soup course for your elegant dinner party; in chilled demitasse cups on a buffet, omitting the condiments and just sprinkling chopped, fresh dill or cilantro (Chinese parsley) on top; or as your main course with attractive sandwiches.

1¾–2 pounds English cucumbers
3 cups chicken stock
3 cups sour cream
3 tablespoons white wine vinegar
1 garlic clove
2 teaspoons salt
⅛ teaspoon white pepper

Wash but do not peel cucumbers. Cut them into 1-inch chunks. Puree all ingredients in an electric blender. The blender jar will not accommodate the entire amount at once, so you will have to refill it several times to achieve the right consistency.

Refrigerate 2–3 hours. Serve in chilled bowls with the following condiments:

1 hard-cooked egg, chopped
1 large tomato, diced
1 avocado, diced
1 bunch green onions, chopped
1 cup croutons

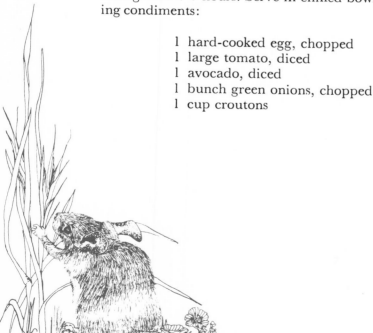

This is such a nice way to begin a dinner party, particularly if you are blessed with a handsome tureen and the appropriate oriental accessories. The visual effect is lovely, though, even without them.

*Serves
12 to 14*

*Preparation
15 minutes*

3 quarts chicken broth
½ cup Mirin (Japanese wine) or dry sherry
3 tablespoons soy sauce

GARNISHES
12–14 fresh mushrooms, thinly sliced
2 lemons, thinly sliced
2 bunches green onions, sliced diagonally into
    ¼-inch thick slivers
1 carrot, sliced paper-thin
½ pound tiny shrimp (optional)

Bring broth to a simmer. Stir in wine and soy sauce. Simmer 5 minutes.

Arrange garnishes on a lacquered tray. Transfer soup to heated tureen. At table, ladle into small, porcelain bowls or mugs and add a little of each garnish.

10 CREAM of LEEK and CHARD SOUP

Serves 8

*Preparation
40 minutes*

This is one of those versatile soups that can be served any time of the year as an entree or first course. Piping hot, it makes a great Sunday supper with FRENCH PEASANT BREAD and a green salad. On a warm, summer evening, omit the ham and serve chilled to begin your dinner party.

1 pound chard (or spinach)
4 large leeks
2½ tablespoons butter
6 tablespoons flour
4½ cups chicken broth
4½ cups water
1 teaspoon salt
1 pound cream cheese, room temperature
2 cups yogurt
4 egg yolks
2 cups cooked ham, chopped
2½ tablespoons butter
Salt and white pepper to taste
½ cup finely chopped chives

Wash chard and finely chop. Remove roots and green stems from leeks and rinse of any sand. Chop.

Melt butter in a heavy soup kettle and add chard and leeks. Cook gently until soft. Sprinkle in flour and cook for 2 minutes over medium-high heat, stirring constantly.

Remove from heat and add chicken broth, water, and salt. Return to low heat and continue to stir until mixture thickens slightly. Simmer for 15 minutes.

Mash cream cheese in a bowl and beat in yogurt and egg yolks until smooth. Sauté ham in remaining 2½ tablespoons butter.

Carefully stir the cheese mixture into the soup and cook over low heat for 5 minutes, stirring constantly. Add ham. Serve garnished with chopped chives.

Light and lovely.

Serves 8

Preparation
15 minutes

Cooking
1 hour

Cool

⅓ cup coarsely chopped parsley
½ cup coarsely chopped celery
¾ cup coarsely chopped onion
¾ cup coarsely chopped carrot
1 pound ground beef
4 egg whites
1 tablespoon black peppercorns
2 bay leaves
½ teaspoon thyme
Salt and pepper to taste
8 cups beef broth
1 cup water
2 cups dry red wine

Combine all vegetables, meat, egg whites, and seasonings in a large, heavy saucepan or Dutch oven. Add broth and water and mix with a wooden spoon. Bring to a boil over high heat, stirring to avoid sticking. The stock will become cloudy and a white foam will form. When the mixture comes to a boil, stop stirring and reduce heat to a simmer. As the soup simmers, a crust will form on the surface with one or two holes through which the liquid will boil gently. Do not disturb these in any way, in order to maintain the clarity of the soup.

After one hour, strain through a sieve lined with 4 layers of cheese cloth that has been wrung out in cold water, taking care not to disturb crust.

Let consommé come to room temperature and refrigerate. When chilled, remove any fat that has formed on top.

When ready to serve, add red wine and reheat.

As a prelude to a rich meal, it is nice to serve this in mugs in the living room.

12 CREAM OF CHESTNUT SOUP

Serves 6 A nice beginning for a special winter evening.

Preparation
30 minutes

1 pound fresh chestnuts, shelled*
2 tablespoons butter
1 large onion, chopped
1 large carrot, chopped
2 cups strong chicken or turkey broth
¾ cup light cream
¼ cup sherry
Salt and pepper to taste
Whipped cream
Paprika
Sherry

*To shell chestnuts, slit convex sides with a sharp knife. Bake in an oiled pan at 450° for 5–6 minutes. When cool enough to handle, remove shells and skins with knife. If fresh chestnuts are not available, you may use an 8 or 10-ounce jar of vacuum-packed chestnuts.

In a heavy pan, melt butter and sauté onions until lightly browned. Add chestnuts, carrots, and stock. If stock is not strong enough, add 1 chicken bouillon cube. Simmer until chestnuts are soft, about 20 minutes.

Puree cooked mixture in blender, processing in small batches until smooth. Combine in a medium-sized sauce pan with cream and sherry and heat to simmer. Do not boil. Salt and pepper to taste.

Top each serving with a dollop of lightly salted, whipped cream and a dash of paprika. Provide a cruet of sherry on the side for those who wish extra flavoring.

This is a very rich soup. You will like it best with roasted meats and poultry.

A beautiful soup. It may be served at a formal dinner of many courses or at the beginning of an elegant luncheon.

*Serves
8 to 10*

> ½ pound ricotta cheese (room temperature)
> 1 whole egg
> 1 egg yolk
> 1 teaspoon salt
> Grating of nutmeg
> ¾ cup freshly grated Parmesan cheese
> 2–2½ quarts chicken broth
> Minced parsley

*Preparation
15 minutes*

*Baking
45 minutes*

Preheat oven to 300°.

Beat the ricotta for several minutes for a more refined texture. Add the egg, egg yolk, salt, nutmeg, and Parmesan cheese. Blend well with a rubber spatula and spread in a buttered, 8 x 8-inch, glass baking dish.

Place the baking dish, uncovered, in a larger pan filled with 1-inch hot water. Bake until firm, about 45 minutes.

Cool the ricotta completely, then cut into very small cubes; the smaller the cube, the more elegant the soup. This may be prepared several days in advance, keeping the cubes covered and refrigerated. When ready to use, the cubes should be at room temperature.

To serve, fill a warmed tureen with piping-hot chicken broth and add the cheese cubes. Sprinkle a little minced parsley on top.

14 FETTUCINE FERRARI

Serves
4 to 6

Preparation
15 minutes

Nice! You may treat this as a first course or as an entree with TOSSED GREEN SALAD and FRENCH PEASANT BREAD. The cherry tomatoes give it extra appeal for a summer supper.

> 1 pound fettuccine
> ½ cup butter
> 1 bunch green onions, chopped
> 1–2 cloves garlic, minced
> 1 cup cherry tomatoes, quartered
> 4 ounces ham, cut in ¼-inch cubes
> 1 egg yolk
> ¼ cup heavy cream
> ½ cup freshly grated Parmesan cheese
> Salt to taste
> Freshly ground pepper to taste

In a large kettle, cook the fettuccine in boiling, salted water until it has reached the "al dente" stage, still firm to the bite. Drain thoroughly.

Melt the butter in a medium skillet. Add the scallions and garlic, cooking gently until onions are tender.

Add the tomatoes and sauté for 1–2 minutes. Add ham to heat through. Beat the egg yolk and then beat the cream into the egg only until well-mixed. Slowly stir into the tomato and ham mixture with a flat whisk and cook just until thickened and well-blended. Add remaining ingredients and remove from heat.

Add the sauce to the hot fettuccine, toss, and serve immediately on warm plates.

CONCHIGLIE means "seashells" in Italian. Its pretty shape makes it an ideal pasta for trapping the tasty morsels of sausage with the delicate sauce, so that each biteful is a pleasure. This particular recipe is very nice as a first course.

Serves 4 to 6

Preparation 20 minutes

> 2 tablespoons chopped shallots
> 2 tablespoons butter
> 2 tablespoons olive oil
> ½ pound luganega sausage,* skinned and crumbled
> 1½ cups heavy cream
> Freshly ground pepper to taste
> Grating of nutmeg
> 1 pound conchiglie, the smaller shells preferred
> Salt to taste
> Chopped parsley
> Freshly grated Parmesan cheese

*Luganega is a mild pork sausage but it may not be readily available in the markets. Bratwurst is a good substitute. Do not use sweet Italian sausage or any seasoned with fennel.

Sauté the shallots in a medium saucepan with the butter and oil until soft. Add the sausage and sauté for 10 minutes, stirring frequently.

Add the cream and freshly ground pepper. Increase the heat to medium and cook, stirring frequently, until the cream has thickened. Add a grating of nutmeg.

Drop the conchiglie into 4 quarts boiling, salted water and stir several times to separate. Cook until "al dente", still firm to the bite, then drain well, tossing gently to empty the shells of any water.

Combine the pasta with the sauce and serve immediately on warmed plates with a sprinkling of parsley on top for color. Pass a bowl of freshly grated Parmesan cheese.

16 PASTA PRIMAVERA

Serves 4–8   A wonderful way to enjoy your garden's bounty.

Preparation
30 minutes

1 bunch broccoli, flowers only
1 bunch asparagus, tips only
1 small zucchini, sliced
1 summer squash, cubed
1 cup cut green beans
½ cup peas
1 pound vermicelli, cooked "al dente"
1 cup thinly sliced mushrooms
1 bunch scallions, chopped
2 cloves garlic, minced
2 tablespoons butter
2 cups cherry tomatoes, cut in halves
¼ cup chopped parsley
2 tablespoons chopped fresh basil (or 1 teaspoon dried)
½ teaspoon dried red pepper flakes (optional)
¼ cup butter
2 tablespoons chicken broth
¾ cup heavy cream
⅔ cup freshly grated Parmesan cheese
Salt and freshly ground pepper to taste
Toasted pine nuts (optional)

Cook the first 6 vegetables, each separately, in boiling salted water until *just* tender. Rinse in cold running water until chilled. Drain well. It is very important that the vegetables remain crisp. This may be done well in advance of preparing the pasta, refrigerating the vegetables in plastic bags.

Place cooked vegetables in a bowl. In a medium-sized skillet, sauté mushrooms, scallions, and garlic in 2 tablespoons butter for 2–3 minutes. Add tomatoes and cook 1 more minute, stirring gently. Add to the bowl of vegetables, along with parsley, basil, and red pepper flakes.

In a large pan or Dutch oven, melt ¼ cup butter. Add chicken broth, cream, cheese, and salt and pepper to taste. Stir with a whisk until smooth but do not boil. Add vegetables only to heat through, then cooked pasta. Check seasoning.

Serve immediately, dividing among heated plates with sprinklings of toasted pine nuts on top. Pass extra cheese.

SPAGHETTI CARBONARA **17**

Great for dinner in ski country!

*Serves
4 to 6*

*Preparation
25 minutes*

8 thick slices bacon, cut in strips, crosswise
1 large onion, thinly sliced
¼ cup dry white wine
3 eggs, lightly beaten
⅔ cup freshly grated Parmesan cheese
2 tablespoons chopped parsley
½ teaspoon salt
Freshly ground pepper to taste
1 pound spaghetti or linguine
Freshly grated Parmesan cheese

In a medium skillet, lightly brown bacon strips and sliced onion. When brown, pour off all but ½ cup of the bacon fat. Add the wine and simmer for 15–20 minutes.

In a bowl, combine the eggs, ⅔ cup Parmesan cheese, parsley, salt, and pepper.

Cook the spaghetti in boiling, salted water until "al dente", still firm to the bite. Drain well.

Toss the spaghetti with egg mixture and then bacon mixture. Supply warm plates for your guests and serve the pasta immediately in a heated bowl. Have extra cheese at hand.

18 A VERY SPECIAL LASAGNE

Serves
12 as pasta
8 as entree

Preparation
1 hour,
15 minutes

Baking
30 minutes

And it really is. It is rich and so delicate in texture and flavors that it becomes an elegant dish for a first course or entree.

½ pound lasagne noodles
1 pound ground beef
½ cup chopped onion
3 cloves garlic, minced
1 tablespoon olive oil
3 pounds tomatoes (6–7 large), peeled, seeded, chopped (or canned tomatoes, drained)
1½ teaspoons seasoned salt
2 tablespoons chopped parsley (or 1 teaspoon dried)
1 teaspoon basil (if you are fortunate enough to have fresh basil, use 2 tablespoons chopped)
½ teaspoon oregano
¼ teaspoon freshly ground pepper

Cook lasagne noodles in boiling, salted water until "al dente", still firm to the bite. Drain and keep them in cold water until ready to use.

Sauté ground beef, onion, and garlic in olive oil until meat is no longer pink. Add remaining ingredients and cook at a fast simmer until sauce is quite thick (about 30–40 minutes). Skim fat. Preheat oven to 400°.

BÉCHAMEL

½ cup butter
4 tablespoons flour
1 cup milk
1 cup chicken broth
1 chicken bouillon cube (optional)
⅛ teaspoon salt

Melt butter, add flour and cook, stirring with a whisk, for one minute. Slowly add milk and chicken broth and bring to a boil, still using whisk. Taste and add chicken bouillon cube, if needed. Add salt.

RICOTTA FILLING

1 egg
½ pound ricotta cheese
¼ cup grated Parmesan cheese
1⁄16–⅛ teaspoon nutmeg
½ teaspoon salt

Beat egg in a bowl. Add remaining ingredients and stir well with a fork.

CHEESES

1½ cups grated Parmesan cheese
4 ounces mozzarella cheese, sliced
4 ounces teleme cheese
Butter

In the following order, layer in a lightly-greased 13 x 9-inch baking dish: a little meat sauce, half of the noodles, half of the remaining meat sauce, ½ cup Béchamel, ½ cup Parmesan cheese, half of the mozzarella, teleme, and ricotta; the remaining noodles and meat sauce, ½ cup Béchamel, ½ cup Parmesan, the remaining mozzarella, teleme, ricotta, Béchamel, and Parmesan cheeses. Dot with butter. At this point, the dish may be covered and refrigerated.

From room temperature, bake at 400°, uncovered, for 30 minutes or more, until bubbly.

This dish freezes very well.

19 QUICHE with WHITE WINE and SHALLOTS

Serves
6 as entree
12 as
1st course

Preparation
15 minutes

Baking
30 minutes

Very delicate and elusive in flavor, this is an appealing quiche for a luncheon. A fresh fruit salad of strawberries, papaya, and pineapple with fingers of BANANA BREAD would complete the menu.

½ cup minced shallots
½ cup dry white wine
6 eggs
1 teaspoon salt
¼ teaspoon white pepper
3 cups heavy cream
Dash of freshly grated nutmeg
12 ounces Gruyère cheese, grated
1 10 x 2-inch pastry shell, baked*

Preheat oven to 400°.

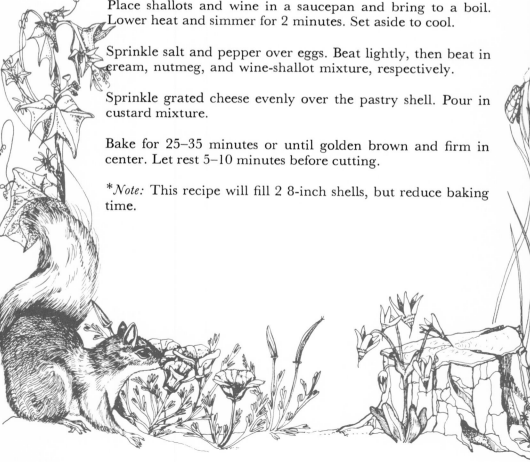

Place shallots and wine in a saucepan and bring to a boil. Lower heat and simmer for 2 minutes. Set aside to cool.

Sprinkle salt and pepper over eggs. Beat lightly, then beat in cream, nutmeg, and wine-shallot mixture, respectively.

Sprinkle grated cheese evenly over the pastry shell. Pour in custard mixture.

Bake for 25–35 minutes or until golden brown and firm in center. Let rest 5–10 minutes before cutting.

Note: This recipe will fill 2 8-inch shells, but reduce baking time.

Dungeness crab and mustard sauce . . . the epitome of good eating to West Coasters. Here is a very nice way to include the equally popular artichoke for a spring or summer luncheon.

Serves 4

Preparation 15 minutes

Cooking 45 minutes

Chilling 3 hours

    1½ tablespoons lemon juice
    1½ tablespoons salad oil
    ½ teaspoon salt
    5 drops Tabasco sauce (optional)
    2 teaspoons minced fresh tarragon leaves (¼ teaspoon dried)
    1 tablespoon finely chopped shallots
    1 pound Dungeness crab meat
    4 large artichokes, cooked

Combine lemon juice, oil, salt, Tabasco, tarragon, and shallots. Add crab meat, mix lightly, and chill. Remove stems and prickly chokes from artichokes and chill.

To serve, fill centers of artichokes with crab. Provide individual bowls of mustard sauce.

    2 egg yolks
    1 tablespoon lemon juice
    1 tablespoon red wine vinegar
    1 teaspoon Dijon mustard
    ½ teaspoon salt
    Dash of pepper
    ½ cup salad oil
    ½ cup plain yogurt

Yield 1½ cups

Preparation 2 minutes

In a blender, place all of the ingredients except oil and yogurt. Blend a few seconds and, with motor still running, add salad oil in a steady stream. In a separate bowl, combine with yogurt and chill.

Serve the stuffed artichokes with sourdough bread and sweet butter, and a bottle of chilled Chablis.

21 AVOCADO CRAB MORNAY

Serves
8 to 10

A beautiful luncheon dish to serve in large scallop shells or ramekins.

Preparation
25 minutes

1/4 cup butter
1/4 cup flour
1 cup light cream
1/2 cup chicken broth
1/2 cup sherry
1/4 cup grated Parmesan cheese
2 tablespoons shredded Swiss or Gruyère cheese
Dash of nutmeg
Dash of cayenne pepper
Dash of salt
6 scallions, minced
1/4 cup butter
3 avocados, peeled, pitted, and diced
1 1/2 pounds crab meat
Freshly grated Parmesan cheese

In a saucepan, melt 1/4 cup butter and stir in flour with a whisk. Add the cream and chicken broth and stir until smooth. Blend in sherry, 1/4 cup Parmesan cheese, Swiss cheese, nutmeg, cayenne pepper, and salt. Remove from heat. At this point, the sauce may be refrigerated, then reheated in a double boiler.

In a large skillet, gently sauté the scallions in 1/4 cup butter until barely limp. Add avocados and crab meat and stir to heat through. Add the sauce and heat, gently stirring, but do not boil.

Mound the crab meat mixture in scallop shells or individual ramekins. Sprinkle with cheese. Bake 5 minutes at 500°. Serve immediately with a pretty green salad and PARTY ROLLS.

Note: Served in smaller shells or individual *au gratin* dishes, it becomes a special first course.

This is a delicate custard baked in a ring mold and filled with creamed seafood, chicken, or sweetbreads . . . exquisite for a ladies' luncheon.

8 eggs
2 cups milk, scalded
1½ teaspoons salt
1 teaspoon onion juice
Pinch of cayenne pepper
3 tablespoons butter
3 tablespoons flour
1½ cups milk
½ pound mushrooms, sliced
2 tablespoons butter
1 pound cooked sweetbreads, chicken, or crab
2 tablespoons sherry
2 teaspoons lemon juice
¼ teaspoon paprika
Salt and pepper to taste

Beat eggs slightly. With a whisk, add the scalded milk, salt, onion juice, and cayenne pepper. Strain the egg mixture through cheese cloth or a fine strainer. Pour into a well-oiled, 8½-inch ring mold. Set in a shallow roasting pan filled with ½-inch hot water. Bake 45 minutes at 300° until firm.

In a large saucepan melt 3 tablespoons butter and stir in flour with a whisk. When blended, add milk, stirring constantly until smooth and thickened. Remove from heat.

In a heavy skillet, sauté mushrooms in 2 tablespoons butter over medium-high heat for 3–5 minutes, or until juices are fairly well-absorbed. Add to cream sauce with seafood, chicken, or sweetbreads. Add sherry, lemon juice, paprika, and salt and pepper to taste. Heat to serve but do not boil.

When egg ring is baked, carefully loosen from mold with a knife and invert on a warm platter. Fill center and surround with creamed mixture. Dress platter with watercress and serve with BRAISED PEAS WITH LETTUCE and PARTY ROLLS.

23 SOW SEE GUY (Coriander Chicken Salad)

Serves 8

Preparation 1 hour

Marinate 1–2 hours

Californian tastes in food are such pleasurable reflections of the diverse and vigorous cultures that have burgeoned here for more than a hundred years. One of the most popular dishes to emerge is SOW SEE GUY, a crisped chicken and shredded lettuce salad that becomes addictive with its bite of coriander. The latter is also known as Chinese parsley, or cilantro as our Mexican friends call it. Do not let the length of this recipe deter you. It is quite easy but you may wish to make it a day ahead, assembling it just before serving as a main dish or buffet salad.

3 whole chicken breasts
¼ cup soy sauce
1 clove garlic, crushed
4 teaspoons sugar
1 tablespoon sherry
2 teaspoons Hoisin Sauce (a thick, spicy sauce available in specialty stores)
1 egg yolk
1 teaspoon soy sauce
6 tablespoons or more sesame seeds
1 cup rice flour
1 cup peanut oil

Marinate the chicken breasts at room temperature in the soy sauce, garlic, sugar, sherry, and Hoisin Sauce for 1–2 hours.

Remove and cut the skins of the marinated chicken into thin strips. With a very sharp knife, slice the chicken into fillets, as thinly as possible, detaching all meat from the bone.

Dip the skin and chicken pieces into egg yolk that has been beaten with 1 teaspoon soy sauce, then into sesame seeds and then rice flour. In a large skillet, fry the chicken in hot peanut oil until crisp and brown. Drain well on paper towels, cool, then refrigerate until ready to serve.

¼ cup sesame oil
¼ cup white vinegar
2 tablespoons soy sauce
2–3 tablespoons sugar
1 teaspoon crushed red pepper
3 cloves garlic, minced
1 green onion, minced
Peanut oil
2 ounces bean thread (also known as long rice,
    rice sticks, rice vermicelli, or cellophane noodles)

Combine the sesame oil, vinegar, soy sauce, sugar, red pepper, garlic, and green onion and reserve as the dressing.

Heat ½-inch of peanut oil in a skillet until very hot. Fry the bean thread, a handful at a time. It will puff up immediately in the hot oil. Quickly remove to paper towels with a slotted spoon. Bean thread may be made a day ahead and covered tightly or it may be frozen.

1 head iceberg lettuce, finely shredded
2 bunches green onions, slivered
1 bunch Chinese parsley, leaves only
1 tablespoon sesame seeds, toasted
¼ cup chopped cashews, almonds, or peanuts

Ten minutes before serving, cut the prepared chicken into thin strips. Combine in a large bowl with the lettuce and remaining ingredients, including the dressing and bean thread, and toss.

24 CHUTNEY CHICKEN SALAD

Serves 8

*Preparation
30 minutes*

It was impossible to decide between these two salads, each excellent in its own right, so we offer both and you may choose.

A very zesty, fresh-tasting salad, it should not be mixed any longer than 2–3 hours before serving.

1 cup mayonnaise
¼–½ cup chutney, chopped
1 teaspoon curry powder
2 teaspoons grated lime peel
¼ cup fresh lime juice
½ teaspoon salt
4 cups diced white meat of chicken or turkey
½ fresh pineapple, cut in bite-sized pieces
½ cup thinly sliced green onions
½ cup slivered almonds, toasted

Combine mayonnaise, chutney, curry powder, lime peel, lime juice, and salt. Toss with other ingredients except almonds. Refrigerate until serving, then sprinkle with almonds.

The wonderful flavors in this salad need time to fully blend, so make it a day ahead.

Serves 8

Preparation 30 minutes

2 cups mayonnaise
2 tablespoons lemon juice
2½ tablespoons Chinese soy sauce
1 rounded tablespoon curry powder
1 tablespoon onion juice
1 tablespoon chutney, chopped
3 cups diced white meat of chicken or turkey
1½ cups chopped celery
1 6-ounce can water chestnuts, drained and sliced
2 cups seedless white grapes
1 1-pound can pineapple chunks, *well*-drained
½ cup slivered almonds, toasted

Combine mayonnaise, lemon juice, soy sauce, curry powder, onion juice, and chutney. Toss with remaining ingredients except almonds. Refrigerate overnight. Sprinkle with almonds.

Note: Either salad may be featured in papaya or pineapple halves or on beds of lettuce with artichoke hearts. Fingers of BANANA BREAD and a light dessert such as LEMON SNOW WITH GRAND MARNIER SAUCE complete the menu.

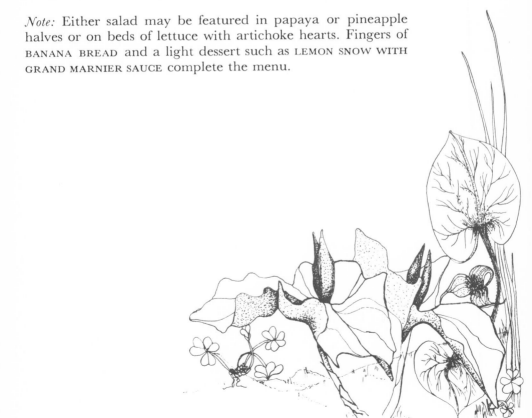

26 SALMON MOUSSE

Marvelous for a summer luncheon!

1 ½ tablespoons unflavored gelatin
¼ cup dry vermouth
1 cup hot sour cream (do not boil)
2 cups cooked salmon (or 1 1-pound can red sockeye salmon)
¼ cup mayonnaise
1 tablespoon lime or lemon juice
2 teaspoons sherry
½ teaspoon anchovy paste
Onion and celery salts to taste
Salt and white pepper to taste
1 cup heavy cream, whipped
½ cup finely chopped celery
2 tablespoons minced onion
1 tablespoon finely chopped parsley
1 tablespoon finely chopped chives

Soften gelatin in vermouth. Dissolve in hot sour cream. Cool.

If necessary, bone and skin salmon. Add to sour cream mixture with mayonnaise, lime juice, sherry, anchovy paste, salts, and pepper. Whirl briefly in an electric blender but do not puree. Refrigerate until mixture begins to congeal.

Into chilled mixture, fold whipped cream, celery, onion, parsley, and chives. Correct seasoning. Pour into a lightly greased, 5-cup ring or fish mold. Chill until firmly set.

Serve with AVOCADO SAUCE and garnish with very thin cucumber and/or lime slices.

2 ripe avocados
1 cup sour cream
1 tablespoon lime juice
1 teaspoon salt
Chopped chives

Puree avocados, sour cream, lime juice, and salt in blender. Serve chilled with a sprinkling of chopped chives.

This peppery, zestful salad makes a gorgeous luncheon entree. Accompany it with CHEESE PUFF GOUGÈRE and finish with a sinfully rich dessert such as FROZEN MOCHA SOUFFLÉ.

Serves 8 to 10

Preparation 15 minutes

Marinate overnight

2–3 avocados
2 pounds large shrimp, peeled and cooked
2 cups salad oil
1 cup cottage cheese
½ medium onion, chopped
½ cup plus 2 tablespoons (5 ounces) white vinegar
Juice of 1 lemon
1 clove garlic
1 teaspoon peppercorns
¼ teaspoon cayenne pepper
1 bunch spinach
1 head romaine lettuce
1 head iceberg lettuce
1 pound bacon, cut in thin strips and fried crisp

Peel and slice the avocados and place in a large bowl with the shrimp.

In an electric blender, combine the oil, cottage cheese, onion, white vinegar, lemon juice, garlic, peppercorns, and cayenne pepper. Pour over the avocados and shrimp and gently mix. Cover and refrigerate overnight.

Wash the greens thoroughly and shake well. Wrap the greens in well-dampened kitchen towels. Refrigerate overnight.

When ready to serve, tear the crisp greens into bite-sized pieces and combine with the avocados, shrimp, and dressing. Toss lightly. Sprinkle crisp bacon bits over the top.

If you wish to serve this as a salad course at dinner, we suggest substituting bay shrimp for the large shrimp.

28 CURRIED SHRIMP

Serves 6

*Preparation
15 minutes*

This is a mild but very flavorful curry dish, making it ideal for a brunch or luncheon and lovely chafing dish fare for large groups. You may prepare the sauce a day ahead.

½ cup minced onion
5 tablespoons butter
5 tablespoons flour
1 teaspoon curry powder
1 teaspoon dry mustard
¼ teaspoon pepper
½ cup chicken broth
½ cup water
2 teaspoons catsup
2 cups milk
3 cups cooked shrimp (crab or chicken may be substituted)

Cook onion in butter until tender. Combine dry ingredients and stir into onion and butter with a whisk. Add broth, water, and catsup, stirring over low heat until warm. Add milk while stirring and cook until smooth and thickened.

Just short of serving time, reheat the sauce and add the shrimp to heat through but do not boil. Provide the following condiments in separate dishes:

1 cup shredded coconut
1 cup toasted whole almonds
1 cup CHUTNEY
1 bunch green onions, chopped
¾ pound bacon, cut in slivers and fried until crisp

For a very pretty buffet, feature a big bowl of fluffy, white rice that has been tossed with butter and chopped parsley, PARTY ROLLS, and a large platter of butter lettuce leaves topped with slices of pink grapefruit and avocados and a celery seed dressing. SUMMER LEMON SOUFFLÉ is just the right ending.

The changes of seasons in northern California are delightfully subtle. Spring is signaled by the pungent odor of fresh, damp earth, the kinetic flutterings of myrtle warblers among the oaks, and a tingling awareness of how really green everything is. With eagerness, one scrubs away winter's rusts from the outdoor grill, readying it for one of the most pleasing of spring dinners . . . fresh salmon.

*Serves
6 to 8*

*Preparation
5 minutes*

*Marinate
2 hours*

*Barbecue
15 minutes*

> 3 large cloves garlic, crushed
> 1 tablespoon salt
> Half of a 10 to 12-pound salmon, boned (or 6–8 salmon steaks)
> 2 tablespoons chopped parsley
> 3 limes
> Branches of rosemary (optional)
> Butter

Combine garlic and salt into a paste and gently rub onto both sides of salmon. Place, skin-side down, in a shallow glass dish or stainless steel pan. Sprinkle with parsley. Squeeze the juice from the limes and add to fish. With a spoon, scrape the pulp from the limes and spread over fish. Marinate at room temperature for 2 hours. Periodically, spoon marinade over fish.

When the coals have turned white in the barbecue, add a branch or two of fresh rosemary and brush the grill with oil. Remove fish from its marinade and place, meat-side down, on hot grill for 5 minutes, then turn it over with spatulas. Scatter a few lumps of butter on top of the fish and barbecue 10–15 minutes more, depending on fire. The fish should just begin to flake when done.

Boiled new potatoes, served in hot butter and chives, and fresh asparagus are ideal companions, with a sauceboat of Hollandaise on the side.

30 HUACHINANGO FRANCESCA (Red Snapper)

A native of Central America, Francesca brought many choice recipes with her, adapting them to the tastes of her California "family". HUACHINANGO is one of their favorites. It is quite simple to prepare, but the instructions should be followed to the letter in order to attain the memorable result.

2–2¼ pounds red snapper fillets
1 teaspoon salt
2 cloves garlic, crushed
¼ cup lime juice
2 tablespoons olive oil
1 medium onion, sliced very thinly
3 pounds tomatoes, peeled, seeded, and chopped
   (or 1 28-ounce can whole tomatoes, drained and chopped)
10–12 pitted green olives, sliced in half
2 fresh jalapeño chilis, seeded and minced*
⅛ teaspoon oregano
⅛ teaspoon thyme
3 bay leaves
2 tablespoons butter
Cilantro (Chinese parsley)

Place the fish in a shallow, glass dish. Make a paste of salt and garlic and gently rub over the fillets. Add lime juice and marinate at room temperature, covered, for at least an hour, preferrably two, turning the fish several times.

About 25 minutes before serving time, heat the oil in a heavy, 11 to 12-inch skillet and gently sauté the onion until translucent, about 3 minutes. Add tomatoes, olives, chilis, oregano, thyme, and bay leaves. Simmer, uncovered, for 10 minutes, stirring occasionally.

Remove the sauce to a bowl to keep warm on back of stove. Add the butter to the same pan over high heat. When it is sizzling but not brown, add fillets, discarding marinade. Maintain high heat, cooking the fillets 2–3 minutes on each side.

As soon as fillets begin to flake, pour the sauce over them, discarding bay leaves, and remove from heat.

Transfer the fish and its sauce to a warmed platter and decorate it with sprigs of cilantro. Serve with buttered, parslied rice and a fresh, green vegetable.

*Note: This dish is at its best when fresh chili peppers are used but if they are unobtainable, you may substitute canned green chilis to taste.

31 CIOPPINO

The credit for this fantastic fish stew goes to the famed Italian fishermen of San Francisco's wharf.

Preparation
30 minutes

Cooking
1 ¼ hours

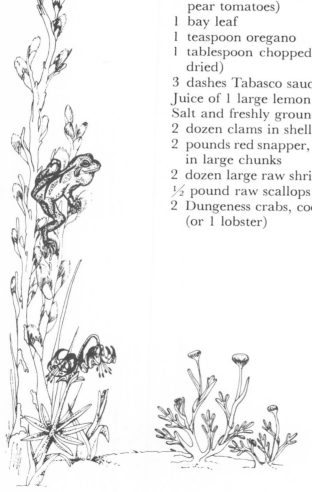

2 large onions, chopped
2 bunches scallions, chopped
2 green peppers, seeded and chopped
4 cloves garlic, minced
¼ cup olive oil
4 tablespoons butter
½ pound fresh, medium mushrooms, quartered
2 cups red wine
1 15-ounce can tomato sauce
3 pounds tomatoes (6–7 large) peeled, seeded and chopped (or 1 1-pound, 12-ounce can Italian pear tomatoes)
1 bay leaf
1 teaspoon oregano
1 tablespoon chopped fresh basil (or 1 teaspoon dried)
3 dashes Tabasco sauce
Juice of 1 large lemon
Salt and freshly ground pepper
2 dozen clams in shell, well-scrubbed
2 pounds red snapper, or any firm-fleshed fish, cut in large chunks
2 dozen large raw shrimp, shelled and deveined
½ pound raw scallops
2 Dungeness crabs, cooked, cleaned, and cracked (or 1 lobster)

In a large kettle, sauté onions, scallions, green peppers, and garlic in oil and butter for 5 minutes or until tender, stirring often. Add mushrooms and sauté 4–5 minutes more. Add wine, tomato sauce, tomatoes, herbs, and Tabasco. Cover and simmer 1 hour or more.

If the sauce has been made ahead of time, reheat 15 minutes before serving time. Add the lemon juice, and salt and freshly ground pepper to taste.

To the heated sauce, add the clams and simmer 3 minutes. Then add snapper, shrimp, and scallops and simmer 3 more minutes or until clams open and shrimp are pink. Do *not* overcook. Add cooked crab or lobster at very last, just to heat through. (You may cook live lobster in CIOPPINO, but add it 5 minutes before the clams. Also, instead of live lobster, you may use 2 frozen lobster tails but cut them in half lengthwise and add them at the same time as the snapper.)

As soon as the crab is heated through, remove the bay leaf, check the seasoning, and serve in large, warmed bowls with chunks of sourdough bread, a great green salad, and a bottle of hearty red wine. Have large napkins or bibs at hand.

Note: The sauce may be made a day or two in advance.

32 SOLE INGE-LISE

Serves
8–10

Preparation
10 minutes

Baking
30 minutes

A beautifully simple and delicious fish course.

> 3 pounds small fillets of sole
> Salt and white pepper
> ½ pound tiny shrimp
> 1 cup chopped leeks
> 2 tablespoons butter
> 1 cup heavy cream
> 4–5 tablespoons tomato paste
> 2½ tablespoons Dijon wine mustard
> 1½ teaspoons cornstarch

Season the fillets with salt and white pepper to taste. Spoon the shrimp onto the fillets and roll up, placing them together in a buttered, shallow, 2-quart casserole.

Sauté the leeks in the butter until limp and spoon over fillets.

Combine the cream, tomato paste, mustard, and cornstarch until well-blended. Pour over the leeks and fish.

At this point, the dish may be refrigerated. Let it reach room temperature before baking, uncovered, at 350° for 30 minutes.

Serve with PARTY ROLLS as a fish course or with fluffy white rice and CELERY WITH ALMONDS as an entree.

A quite different and nicely exotic sole.

Serves 4

*Preparation
10 minutes*

4 medium fillets of sole (about 1½ pounds)
¼ cup flour
1 teaspoon paprika
1 teaspoon salt
¼ teaspoon white pepper
⅓ cup butter
½ cup dry white wine
½ teaspoon ginger
2 tablespoons lemon juice
2 tablespoons brown sugar
2 bananas, cut in quarters lengthwise
2–3 ounces toasted, slivered almonds (optional)

Dip fillets in mixture of flour, paprika, salt, and white pepper.

Melt butter in a large skillet and brown fillets for 2–3 minutes on each side over medium heat. Remove to a warm platter.

Combine wine, ginger, lemon juice, and brown sugar in skillet. Add bananas and raise heat to medium-high. Cook 2 minutes, spooning the sauce over the bananas.

To serve, cover fillets with bananas and sauce. Sprinkle with toasted almonds. Keep the rest of your menu simple with just fluffy, white rice and a fresh green vegetable or salad.

34 CHICKEN with CASHEWS and BROCCOLI

Serves 6

*Preparation
20 minutes*

This is a very pretty and flavorful oriental dish, and fun to prepare.

1 tablespoon cornstarch
1 cup chicken broth
3 tablespoons dry sherry
2 tablespoons soy sauce
¼–½ teaspoon Tabasco sauce
¼ cup peanut oil
3 chicken breasts, skinned, boned, cut into 1-inch chunks
2 slices fresh ginger (½ teaspoon powdered)
3 cups broccoli flowerets
1 medium, sweet red pepper, cut in 1-inch squares
½ pound mushrooms, sliced
1 bunch scallions, slivered
1 clove garlic, minced
⅓ cup dry roasted cashews

In oriental fashion, assemble all of your ingredients ahead of time. Combine the cornstarch, chicken broth, sherry, soy sauce, and Tabasco in a small bowl and have ready.

Ten minutes before serving, heat the oil in a hot skillet or wok. When oil is very hot, add chicken and ginger. Cook, stirring constantly, until chicken turns white. If using a skillet, remove chicken and discard ginger slices. If using a wok, just remove ginger slices and push chicken up sides.

Place the broccoli, red pepper, mushrooms, scallions, and minced garlic in the skillet or center of wok. Cook 3 minutes, stirring constantly.

Combine the chicken and the cornstarch mixture with the vegetables and continue stirring until the sauce thickens slightly. Sprinkle with the cashews and serve immediately with steaming hot rice. Don't forget the chopsticks!

A good salad with this dish would be slices of navel oranges and red onions arranged over butter lettuce leaves and served with WATERCRESS SAUCE.

The creator of CHICKEN BREASTS ALLA MARGHERITA is a member of one of northern California's oldest Italian families. Her celebrated flair and elegance in entertaining are reflected not only by this splendid dish, but her MINESTRINA DI CUBETTI, RISOTTO ALLA MILANESE, and ZABAGLIONE. Each one is special.

Serves 6

Preparation
20 minutes

Baking
15 minutes

3 large chicken breasts
¼ cup flour
1 teaspoon salt
⅛ teaspoon freshly ground pepper
4 tablespoons butter
2 ounces Prosciutto slices
4 ounces Fontina cheese, thinly sliced
½ cup white wine
½ cup chicken broth
1 tablespoon brandy (optional)

Preheat oven to 350°.

Remove skin and slice 2–3 fillets from each side of a breast. Combine the flour, salt, and pepper, and lightly dredge the fillets. Heat the butter in a heavy skillet. Cook the fillets slowly over medium-low heat for 2–3 minutes. Do not overcook. Remove them to a shallow, 2-quart, glass baking dish. On each piece of chicken, arrange a thin slice of Prosciutto and top with a thin slice of Fontina cheese.

Into the brown juices of the pan, stir the wine, chicken broth, and brandy. Simmer until the liquid is reduced and slightly thickened, about 5 minutes. Pour into the baking dish with the breasts. At this point, it may be refrigerated until 15–20 minutes before serving.

Bake, uncovered, for 15 minutes or until hot and bubbly. Delicious served with RISSOTTO ALLA MILANESE and a fresh, green vegetable such as buttered spinach accented with a grating of nutmeg.

36 WATERZOOIE van KIP (Belgian Chicken Soup)

Serves 8

Preparation 20 minutes

Cooking 1 ¼ hours

Given by a Belgian friend, this is a specialty in her country. It is surprisingly easy to prepare, providing flavors to which we are all accustomed but combining them in a new and different way. Perfect for a Sunday supper with guests.

2 2½–3 pound broiling chickens, cut into serving pieces
Salt and freshly ground pepper
1 tablespoon butter
2 leeks, finely chopped
2 celery stalks, finely chopped
3 carrots, peeled and sliced
1 large onion, finely chopped
¼ cup finely chopped parsley
4–5 cups chicken broth, heated
2 pinches mace (optional)
4 egg yolks
¼ cup chopped parsley for garnish
Thin lemon slices (optional)

Salt and pepper chicken pieces. Use 1 tablespoon butter to thoroughly grease the bottom of a Dutch oven or a heavy, heat-proof casserole. Layer leeks, celery, carrots, onion, and parsley in the casserole. Arrange chicken pieces on top. Tightly cover the casserole and simmer over low heat for 10 minutes. Don't worry! It will not burn if properly covered and temperature is kept low.

Add hot broth and mace, cover, and simmer 1 hour. Remove chicken pieces and keep warm while preparing the sauce. Skim fat from remaining broth. Beat egg yolks lightly and add to the hot broth and vegetables, stirring constantly. Immediately remove from heat.

To serve, divide the broth and vegetables among 8 warm, shallow, soup bowls. Top with pieces of chicken and garnish with chopped parsley. Thin lemon slices would be a nice, extra touch. You need only hot, crusty French bread and a green salad to complete the meal.

A prominent San Francisco family's revered cook of many years prepared this often for the loveliest of dinner parties. It is easy and foolproof, but be sure to use only the finest white veal.

*Serves
4 to 6*

*Preparation
10 minutes*

*Roasting
4 hours*

> 1 small, boned, rolled leg of veal
> ½ cup butter, melted
> 1 8-ounce jar Dijon wine mustard
> 1 10½-ounce can consommé
> ¼ cup sherry
> Chopped parsley

Preheat oven to 300°.

Place meat in a shallow roasting pan. Blend melted butter and mustard and pour over meat, covering all sides.

Roast 4 hours. During the last hour, baste every 20 minutes with a mixture of consommé and sherry.

The meat will carve more easily if you wait 20 to 30 minutes after removing it from the oven, keeping it warm on the back of the stove with a loose cover of foil.

Make a gravy of the pan juices, thickening, if necessary, with arrowroot or flour. Pass gravy separately with chopped parsley sprinkled on top.

CARROT SOUFFLÉ and fresh asparagus spears with Hollandaise are just right with this.

38 OSSOBUCO

Serves 6

Preparation 45 minutes

Cooking 1¼ hours

Although OSSOBUCO may be regarded as simple fare by some, it is far from it with its lovely blend of flavors and hidden treasures of delicate marrow. We like this version of the popular Milanese dish very much.

4 tablespoons butter
1 large onion, finely chopped
1 stalk celery, finely chopped
2 carrots, thinly sliced
1 clove garlic, minced
4 veal hind-shanks, cut in 2-inch pieces
Flour
Salt and freshly ground white pepper
½ cup oil
1 cup dry white wine
2 cups chicken broth
2 cups drained, canned, Italian pear tomatoes, chopped (28-ounce can)
1 teaspoon marjoram
½ teaspoon salt
Freshly ground white pepper

¼ cup finely chopped parsley
1 tablespoon finely chopped lemon peel
1 teaspoon finely chopped orange peel
1 clove garlic, minced
Salt and freshly ground white pepper

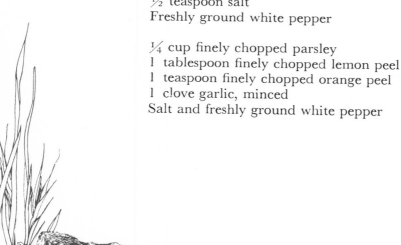

In a large, heavy pot or Dutch oven, melt butter and add the onion, celery, carrots, and garlic. Cook gently over low heat until they are soft and golden, about 10 minutes. In the meantime, dredge the veal shanks with flour seasoned with salt and white pepper. In a heavy skillet over medium-high heat, brown the shanks in hot oil on all sides and transfer to the vegetables.

Add the white wine, chicken stock, tomatoes, marjoram, salt, and white pepper. Cover and simmer very slowly for 1¼ to 1½ hours, or until the veal is fork-tender. This may also be done in a 325° oven for the same length of time. You may prepare this recipe to this point hours ahead of time and reheat gently before serving.

When the shanks are cooked, remove them from the broth and place them in a shallow roasting pan in a 450° oven for 5 to 10 minutes to finish. In the meantime, reduce the broth over high heat, skimming fat and thick foam from the center as the liquid boils. When the broth is about half its original amount, remove from heat and stir in the parsley, lemon and orange peel, and garlic. Taste and add more salt and white pepper, if necessary. Serve the gravy over the shanks or pass separately.

Traditionally, OSSOBUCO is served with RISOTTO alla MILANESE. We also recommend sliced zucchini. A simple preparation is to gently sauté chopped onion in a little butter in a heavy skillet for 2 minutes. Add sliced zucchini and salt and pepper to taste. Tightly cover and simmer until just tender, from 5 to 10 minutes.

39 MEDALLIONS of PORK VERACRUZ

Serves 6

*Preparation
30 minutes*

The orange and wine flavors are magical with the pork, transforming it into an elegantly beautiful entree.

 3 pork tenderloins
 2 teaspoons dry mustard
 1 teaspoon salt
 ¼ teaspoon freshly ground pepper
 2 tablespoons butter
 2–3 cloves garlic, minced
 ½ cup dry vermouth
 ½ cup white wine
 ¾–1 cup orange juice
 1 tablespoon flour
 2 tablespoons water
 Minced parsley
 Zests of orange rind
 Orange slices

Trim fat and sinew from loins and cut in ½-inch thick slices. Combine dry mustard, salt, and pepper, and lightly rub into meat.

In a large, heavy skillet, melt butter over medium-high heat and add pork slices and garlic. Brown the meat for 3–5 minutes on each side. Add the vermouth, wine, and orange juice, and reduce heat. Simmer, covered, for 8–10 minutes or until meat is tender. Remove the medallions to a warm plate and cover.

Make a paste of the flour and water. With a flat whisk, stir the paste into the pan juices and simmer to thicken.

When ready to serve, return the medallions to the hot pan gravy for a minute then arrange on a warmed serving platter, and cover with the gravy.

Sprinkle with minced parsley and zests of orange rind, placing sprigs of parsley and slices of orange around the platter. For great eye and taste appeal, serve with a MUSHROOM-RICE RING filled with buttered sugar snap peas or Chinese pea pods.

A hearty Greek dish that lends itself so well to a cozy supper on a wintry night.

Serves 6

Preparation 20 minutes

Cooking 1 ½ hours

3 pounds lamb shoulder, or 2-pounds boned, cut into cubes*
2 tablespoons olive oil
Salt and pepper
3 small onions, chopped
4 celery stalks, chopped
3 carrots, cut in 1-inch pieces
1 clove garlic, minced
2 cups water
Salt and pepper to taste
4 eggs separated
¼ cup lemon juice

In a large skillet, brown the meat quickly in hot oil, adding some salt and pepper. Add the onions, reduce heat, and cook until transparent.

Transfer the browned meat and the onions to a Dutch oven or stewing pot. Add celery, carrots, garlic, and water, plus more salt and pepper, if needed Simmer, covered, 1–1 ½ hours or until the meat is tender. Add a little water from time to time, if needed. Remove from heat, skim fat, and cool slightly.

Just before serving, beat the egg whites until they form peaks. Gradually beat in yolks. Slowly add lemon juice, continuing to beat. Pour over the slightly cooled stew and serve at once with buttered rice or noodles, green salad, and a hot crusty bread.

Note: Boned meat is more refined but not nearly so flavorful.

41 LAMB CURRY

Serves 8

Preparation
30 minutes

This is a splendid curry, the coconut milk adding intrigue. If possible, make it early in the day so that all of the flavors may develop.

4 tablespoons curry powder
½ teaspoon ginger
½ teaspoon turmeric
¼ teaspoon paprika
¼ teaspoon cayenne pepper
½ teaspoon salt
¼ teaspoon freshly ground pepper
2½ pounds boned lamb shoulder, cut in ¾-inch
    cubes (or 5 cups cooked lamb)*
6 tablespoons butter
2 onions, chopped
2 stalks celery, chopped
1 green pepper, seeded and chopped
1 clove garlic, minced
2 tart apples, cored and chopped
½ cup seedless raisins
2 tablespoons flour
1 cup chicken broth
2 cups coconut milk**
4 tablespoons mango chutney
Salt to taste
6–8 tablespoons yogurt

Combine the curry powder, ginger, turmeric, paprika, cayenne pepper, salt, and freshly ground pepper, and set aside.

If using raw lamb, sauté the meat in butter until brown. Remove the meat and sauté the onions, celery, green pepper, and garlic in the same pan. While they are cooking, add half of the curry mixture to the vegetables.

When the vegetables are tender, add the apples and raisins. Sprinkle with the flour and stir in the chicken broth and coconut milk. Add more of the curry mixture until the sauce has reached the desired pungency. Add the browned meat and simmer, uncovered, for 10–15 minutes or until meat is tender. Blend in the chutney and salt to taste. Remove from heat and stir in yogurt.

Hot buttered rice and a simple green salad are all that are needed, for the drama of the menu will be focused on the array of condiments. Have fun making a colorful selection from the following: *chutney, preserved kumquats, crumbled crisp bacon, fresh bean sprouts, dried banana chips, shredded coconut, orange slices, avocado chunks, chopped scallions, toasted almonds* or *peanuts, sliced raw mushrooms,* chunks of *fresh tomatoes,* and *hard-boiled eggs* (yolks and whites kept separate).

Note: If using left-over lamb, add 10 minutes after the coconut milk and simmer a few minutes to heat through.

**To make coconut milk, either place the meat of 1 coconut in a blender with 2 cups hot milk, or use 1 cup dried, shredded coconut to 2 cups hot milk. Puree well and strain through cheesecloth.

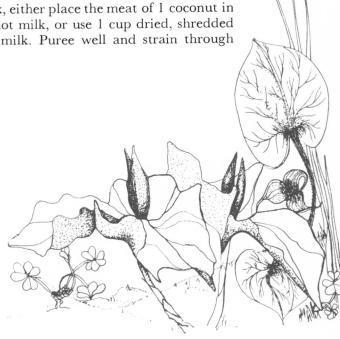

42 SPRING LAMB CHOPS

Serves 6
An elegant entree for an intimate dinner.

Preparation
10 minutes

Standing
1 hour

Cooking
5–10 minutes

12 single-rib lamb chops (very young lamb pre-
    ferred)*
½ cup freshly grated Parmesan cheese
2 eggs, lightly beaten
1 cup fine, dry, bread crumbs
Vegetable oil
Salt
Freshly ground pepper

*Ask your butcher to remove all bone but the rib from the chops.

Turn the chops in the grated cheese, coating both sides. Gently shake away any excess. Immediately dip them in the beaten eggs. Drain the chops of extra egg and turn them in the bread crumbs, coating both sides but shaking free of excess.

At this point, the chops may stand at room temperature for an hour or so, or be refrigerated for 3–4 hours. They must return to room temperature, though, before frying.

Ten minutes before serving time, heat about ¼-inch of oil in a large skillet over medium heat. When it is very hot, fry as many chops as will fit loosely in the skillet. When they have formed a nice crust on one side, season with salt and pepper and turn, seasoning again.

It should take about 4–5 minutes to fry each panful of chops. When done, transfer them to a heated platter with gorgeous clumps of watercress. We suggest RISOTTO ALLA MILANESE with broiled tomato halves and FRESH GREEN BEANS.

It tastes as superb as its aroma.

Serves 6

1 leg of lamb, well-trimmed of fat
Salt
¼ cup finely chopped parsley
3 tablespoons fresh rosemary (1 tablespoon dried)
1 tablespoon olive oil
2 garlic cloves, crushed
¼ teaspoon salt
1¼ cups chicken broth

*Preparation
10 minutes*

*Roasting
2 ½ hours*

Preheat oven to 325°.

Rub entire leg with salt. With a small knife, make 6 or 7 deep incisions in thickest parts of meat.

Combine remaining ingredients except broth and gently push mixture into incisions with fingers and the handle of a teaspoon. Spread any leftover mixture over surface of meat.

Roast for 2½ hours, basting frequently with chicken broth.

Serve with pan-roasted new potatoes and BRAISED PEAS WITH LETTUCE. To prepare potatoes, peel and boil 10–15 minutes or until barely tender. Drain well and place in pan with lamb at least 1 hour before meat is done. Baste with drippings, turning once or twice during roasting.

44 BUTTERFLIED LEG OF LAMB

Serves
6 to 8

Preparation
20 minutes

Marinate
8 hours

Cooking
30–45 minutes

This particular cut of lamb has become a great favorite. It is so adaptable to different kinds of entertaining that menu-planning is a breeze.

1 6–7 pound leg of lamb, butterflied
1 cup dry red wine
¾ cup beef broth
3 tablespoons orange marmalade
2 tablespoons red wine vinegar
1 tablespoon minced dried onion
1 tablespoon dried marjoram
1 tablespoon dried rosemary
1 large bay leaf, crumbled
1 teaspoon seasoned salt
¼ teaspoon ginger
1 clove garlic, crushed

Place lamb in a shallow roasting pan, fat side down. Combine remaining ingredients in a 2-quart saucepan and simmer, uncovered, for 20 minutes. Pour the hot mixture over the lamb and marinate at room temperature for 6–8 hours, turning frequently.

BARBECUE METHOD: Place meat over medium-hot coals, fat side up, for 30 to 45 minutes. Turn several times, being careful not to pierce meat. Periodically brush with marinade.

OVEN METHOD: Preheat oven to 425°. Place meat, fat side up, under broiler, about 4 inches from heat. Broil 10 minutes per side. Transfer meat to preheated oven for 15 minutes.

On a slight diagonal, carve meat in fairly thin slices. Serve with WILD RICE IN A CASSEROLE and BROCCOLI CANTONESE.

Decorative and delicious, these bring a touch of refinement to barbecuing while maintaining a zesty, full-bodied flavor.

Serves 4

*Preparation
10 minutes*

*Marinate
8 hours*

> 2 pounds flank steak
> ¾ cup salad oil
> ½ cup soy sauce
> 2 tablespoons honey
> 2 tablespoons vinegar
> 1 ½ teaspoons ginger
> 1 teaspoon garlic powder
> 1 scallion, finely chopped

Cut steak widthwise into ½-inch strips. Roll up each strip and secure with round toothpicks. Rolls should be approximately 3 inches in diameter.

Combine remaining ingredients in electric blender. Marinate steak rolls in sauce for at least 8 hours.

Barbecue over glowing coals about 5 minutes on each side for medium-rare, or until done to your liking. To broil in your oven, allow about 2 minutes on each side for medium rare.

We particularly like BARLEY AND PINE NUT PILAF and ZUCCHINI with these. Try WALNUT PIE for the finale.

Serves
4 to 6

Preparation
30 minutes

Very much like a Stroganoff, this does take some last-minute preparation, but it is well-worth it. An ideal recipe for a wok, arrange all of your ingredients and make the sauce ahead of time. Thus, you will need to leave your guests for only a short time.

Cooking
15 minutes

1 teaspoon dry mustard
1 teaspoon Dijon wine mustard
½ cup cold water
Pinch of sugar
2 tablespoons flour
1 cup créme fraîche (or ½ cup sour cream and ½ cup light cream)
½ pound fresh mushrooms
2 tablespoons butter
½ teaspoon salt
⅛ teaspoon freshly ground pepper
4 tablespoons butter
1 tablespoon oil
2 pounds beef tenderloin*
Salt and pepper
3 tablespoons minced shallots
1 clove garlic, minced
½ cup strong beef stock
2 tablespoons finely minced dill (or 2 teaspoons dried dill)

*Your butcher should be able to provide you with the tail of the tenderloin, a much less expensive cut of meat and yet just as tender and flavorful. It should be cut in thin strips, 2 inches long.

In a small bowl, combine the 2 mustards with the water and sugar. Let the mixture stand for 30 minutes to develop flavor.

Add the flour to the mustard mixture and blend well with a whisk. Add the créme fraîche and set aside.

Use only the mushroom caps and slice thinly. Melt 2 tablespoons of butter in a small skillet. When it is hot, add the mushrooms and season with salt and pepper. Cook over medium-high heat only until the butter separates from the mushrooms and becomes clear and golden. Immediately remove from heat and set aside.

Approximately 15 minutes before dinner is to be served, melt 4 tablespoons butter with 1 tablespoon oil in a wok or heavy 12-inch skillet. When very hot, sauté the tenderloin strips, a few at a time, over very high heat. Do not crowd the pan. The strips should be browned but still a little rare inside. As each batch is done, remove meat from skillet and reserve, sprinkling with salt and pepper to taste.

Add the shallots and garlic to the wok or skillet and cook over medium heat until soft but not browned. Add beef stock and simmer to reduce by one-third. Add the cream and mustard mixture and stir with a whisk until the broth takes on a velvety appearance.

Add the mushrooms and dill and toss with all of the meat in the broth just to heat through. Taste for seasoning.

Serve in a chafing dish with noodles or rice, a tossed green salad, and FRENCH PEASANT BREAD.

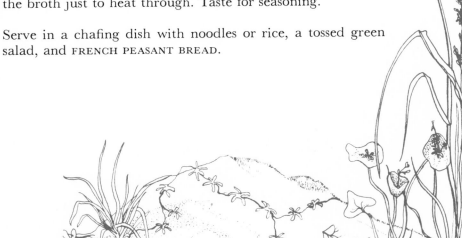

47 TENDERLOIN en BROCHETTE

Serves 8

*Preparation
1 hour*

A superb recipe, it is particularly so served on wild rice with GINGERED PAPAYAS. Do not be concerned by the preparation time. That is due to the amount of handwork which, together with the sauce, may be done in the morning.

BROCHETTES

1–1½ green peppers, cut into 32 1-inch squares
32 1-inch diameter button mushrooms
3 pounds beef tenderloin, cut into 32 1½-inch cubes
6 strips lean bacon, cut into 32 pieces
Olive oil
Salt and freshly ground pepper

Parboil green pepper squares in salted water for one minute. Clean mushrooms, leaving stems even with bases of caps.

On eight 10-inch-long skewers, spear meat, green pepper, bacon, and mushrooms in that order, and repeat until you have 4 pieces of everything on each skewer.

Brush skewers generously with olive oil to coat vegetables and meat, then salt and pepper. Barbecue or broil, turning once, about 5 minutes each side.

SAUCE

4 ounces butter
2 celery stalks, cut in 2-inch lengths
1 small carrot, cut in 2-inch lengths
1 small onion, coarsely chopped
2 teaspoons pickling spices
Pinch or two of dried rosemary
8 ounces tomato sauce
1 cup strong beef stock
1 cup dry red wine
Juice of 2 lemons
4 cloves garlic, minced
Pinch or two of nutmeg
4 egg yolks, well-beaten
Salt and pepper to taste

In a heavy, 10-inch skillet, melt butter and sauté vegetables with the pickling spices and rosemary until well-browned. Add tomato sauce, beef stock, wine, lemon juice, garlic, and nutmeg. Bring to a boil and let liquid reduce to half. Strain through a sieve, discarding solids.

If making ahead, refrigerate sauce at this point and finish just before broiling brochettes.

To finish, add sauce to the well-beaten egg yolks, beating in with a whisk. Reheat, but do not boil, stirring until thickened. Salt and pepper to taste. Keep hot.

SERVING SUGGESTION: Place a spoonful of WILD RICE on each heated dinner plate and sprinkle with Parmesan cheese. Place a brochette on top of each bed of rice, holding meat down with a fork while withdrawing skewer. Cover with sauce and sprinklings of chopped parsley. Serve with GINGERED PAPAYAS and FRESH GREEN BEANS.

48 BEEF BOURGUIGNON

Serves 24

Preparation 1–1½ hours

Baking 3 hours

This is BEEF BOURGUIGNON at its best. We suggest that you make it a day or two ahead so that the flavors may fully develop. A refined stew, it is great for large, winter parties or a gathering after a football game.

10 pounds beef chuck, cut in 1½-inch pieces
1½ cups flour
4 teaspoons salt
1 teaspoon pepper
½ cup butter
½ cup olive oil
¾ cup cognac, warmed
1 pound bacon, diced
6 cloves garlic, mashed
8 carrots, coarsely chopped
4 leeks, coarsely chopped
4 large, yellow onions, chopped
¼ cup chopped parsley
3 bay leaves (or 1 per casserole)
1½ teaspoons thyme
4 tablespoons tomato paste
7 cups burgundy wine
6 cups beef broth or more
Salt and freshly ground pepper
60 small white onions, preferably no wider than an inch
½ cup butter
2 tablespoons sugar
3 pounds button mushrooms
½ cup butter
Juice of 1 lemon
½ cup chopped parsley
Additional salt and freshly ground pepper to taste

Combine flour, salt, and pepper, and dredge meat. In a large, heavy skillet, over high heat, brown meat on all sides in butter and oil. This will have to be done in several batches, adding butter and oil as needed.

As meat is browned, place it in 2 5-quart casseroles or 1 large, deep roasting pan. De-glaze skillet by pouring warmed cognac into it, lighting the cognac with a match, and stirring to loosen particles. Pour over meat.

To the same skillet, add the bacon, garlic, carrots, leeks, chopped onions, and parsley. Cook, stirring, until bacon and vegetables are lightly browned. Add bay leaves, thyme, and tomato paste to skillet, stir, and add all to beef. Add wine and enough beef broth to barely cover meat and mix well. Taste for salt and pepper.

Cover casseroles and bake 2 hours at 350°. Stir occasionally and add more beef broth if necessary.

Peel the white onions by dropping them in boiling water for 1 minute. Cut off the ends and slip off the outer skin. Sauté the white onions in ½ cup butter with the sugar, shaking the pan to caramelize the onions as evenly as possible. Pour a small amount of broth or water over them and simmer, covered, for 10–15 minutes, until they are barely tender.

Sauté the mushrooms in ½ cup butter until lightly browned. Sprinkle with lemon juice. Add mushrooms and onions to beef and cook 1 more hour, or until the beef is tender.

Skim any fat from the surface of the casseroles and remove bay leaves. It is important to again taste for salt and freshly ground pepper. If not serving immediately, refrigerate, removing hardened fat before reheating. When serving, sprinkle with chopped parsley.

BAKED HUNGARIAN NOODLES, FRENCH PEASANT BREAD, and TOSSED GREEN SALAD will be all that you'll need to serve with this.

Note: The BOURGUIGNON freezes beautifully.

49 BEEF WELLINGTON

Serves
8 to 10

Preparation
45 minutes

Baking
20 minutes
30 minutes

There are many nice variations of the popular and impressive BEEF WELLINGTON, but this one excels in all three areas of taste, appearance, and ease of preparation. It may be made ahead of time and will assure success for even the amateur. We are not including the pastry recipe since you may purchase excellent frozen puff paste at your market or use a basic recipe from any quality cookbook.

4 pounds whole beef tenderloin
2 tablespoons soft butter
2 tablespoons brandy
Salt and pepper
1 pound fresh mushrooms
2 teaspoons lemon juice
4 tablespoons butter
½ cup finely chopped scallions
½ cup dry sherry
½ cup minced parsley
Salt and pepper to taste
2 pounds puff pastry
1 egg, beaten
1 tablespoon water

PREBAKING MEAT: Preheat oven to 425°. Tie heavy string at several points around tenderloin to maintain its shape while baking. Place on rack, fat side up, in a shallow roasting pan. Mix 2 tablespoons soft butter with brandy and spread over top and sides. Sprinkle with salt and pepper. Bake 20 minutes.

When done, remove meat to another rack to cool. Let stand until barely warm to touch, about 30 minutes. Remove string and pat dry with a paper towel. Trim away any thick fat.

MUSHROOM FILLING (DUXELLES): Finely chop mushrooms and sprinkle immediately with lemon juice to maintain their light color. In a small skillet, melt the remaining 4 tablespoons butter and add mushrooms, scallions, dry sherry, and parsley. Cook, stirring with a wooden spoon, until the onion is tender and all liquid is absorbed. Salt and pepper to taste. Cool.

ASSEMBLING WELLINGTON: On a pastry cloth or lightly floured board, roll out pastry into a rectangle about ⅜-inch thick. It should be large enough to encase the meat, at least 12 x 18 inches. Spread the duxelles over pastry, pressing in firmly. Leave an inch margin on all sides. Place meat, top side down, in middle of pastry. Wrap pastry around meat and seal seams and ends securely, moistening edges with water if necessary. Place on an ungreased baking sheet, seam side down.

Roll out left-over pastry and cut out small designs to suit your creativity: flowers, stars, holly, etc. Use them to decorate the top of the Wellington. Wrap the Wellington in plastic film and refrigerate until 1 hour before baking.

FINAL BAKING: Let the Wellington stand at room temperature 1 hour before baking.

Preheat oven to 400°. Mix beaten egg and water and brush over all of pastry to ensure a high gloss. Bake the Wellington for 30–35 minutes or until pastry is golden brown. Let stand 15 minutes before placing on a warmed serving platter. Garnish attractively with parsley or watercress.

Carve the Wellington in ¾-inch slices and accompany it with a gravy boat of ROSSINI SAUCE. To complete the menu, we suggest a carrot dish or CELERY ALMONDINE, fresh asparagus or broccoli in lemon butter, and PARTY ROLLS.

50 TENDERLOIN DELUXE

For your most distinguished guests!

3 pounds whole beef tenderloin
2 tablespoons softened butter
¼ cup chopped scallions
2 tablespoons butter
2 tablespoons soy sauce
1 teaspoon Dijon wine mustard
Dash of ground pepper
¾ cup dry sherry

For best results, the meat should sit at room temperature for 2–3 hours before roasting.

Preheat oven to 400°.

Spread the tenderloin with the softened butter. Place on a rack in a shallow roasting pan and bake, uncovered, for 20 minutes.

Meanwhile, sauté the scallions in the remaining butter until tender. Add the soy sauce, mustard, and pepper. Stir in the sherry and heat just until boiling.

When the meat has baked 20 minutes, pour the sauce over it and bake another 20–25 minutes to serve medium-rare. Baste frequently.

Remove from oven and let sit for 10 minutes, then carve in 1-inch slices, overlapping them attractively on a warm platter lavished with parsley. Either feature the tenderloin in its own sauce or offer MUSHROOMS IN WINE SAUCE and a Bearnaise sauce in separate gravy boats.

ROSSINI SAUCE **51**

½ cup butter
3 tablespoons flour
1 cup beef stock
5 peppercorns
1 bay leaf
1 clove
2 tablespoons brandy
2 tablespoons red wine

Serves 10

*Preparation
10 minutes*

In a sauce pan, melt butter and stir in flour with a whisk. Brown. Stir in beef stock until smooth. Add the remaining ingredients and simmer 5 minutes. Remove the bay leaf and clove before serving. Serve with BEEF WELLINGTON.

MUSHROOMS in WINE SAUCE **52**

A very nice sauce for TENDERLOIN DELUXE or BEEF WELLINGTON.

*Serves
8 to 10*

*Preparation
15 minutes*

6 tablespoons butter
½ pound mushrooms, sliced
2 medium onions, finely chopped
1 clove garlic, minced
2 tablespoons chili sauce
1 tablespoon Escoffier Diable Sauce (available in any specialty market)
½ teaspoon flour
Pinch dried marjoram
Pinch dried thyme
4 drops Tabasco sauce
2 dashes Worcestershire sauce
5 ounces dry red wine
1 bouillon cube, dissolved in ¼ cup water
Salt and freshly ground pepper to taste
Minced parsley

Melt the butter in a large skillet. Add the mushrooms, onions, and garlic. Sauté until the onions are soft. Add remaining ingredients and mix well. Barely simmer for about 10 minutes. Serve hot in a gravy boat with a sprinkling of minced parsley.

53 BAKED HUNGARIAN NOODLES

Serves 24

*Preparation
15 minutes*

*Baking
30 minutes*

This recipe has been written to serve 24 guests because it is so suitable for BEEF BOURGUIGNON, but it can easily be divided by 4 to serve 6. Do note that it may be made well in advance of the party.

1 pound fine noodles
4 cups cream-style cottage cheese
4 cups sour cream
1 cup minced onion
3–4 cloves garlic, minced
4 tablespoons Worcestershire sauce
4 dashes Tabasco sauce
4 tablespoons poppy seeds
2 teaspoons salt
Freshly ground pepper to taste
Paprika
Freshly grated Parmesan cheese

Cook noodles in boiling, salted water until tender. Drain. Combine the noodles with the remaining ingredients except the paprika and Parmesan cheese.

Approximately 30 minutes before serving, bake in buttered casseroles at 350° until hot.

Sprinkle with paprika and serve with Parmesan cheese.

We have seen this recipe published several times over the years. Thus, it would not have been considered for this book, but it is so outstanding with roast beef and grilled meats that we were compelled to make the exception.

Serves 8–10

Preparation 25 minutes

Baking 35 minutes

    1 quart milk
    ½ cup butter
    1 cup hominy grits (either regular or quick-cooking)
    1 teaspoon salt
    ⅛ teaspoon pepper
    ⅓ cup butter, melted
    6 ounces Gruyére cheese, grated
    ⅓ cup freshly grated Parmesan cheese

In a heavy, 3-quart saucepan, bring milk to a boil. Add ½ cup butter, cut in pieces for quicker melting. Gradually stir in the grits. Resume the boil and continue cooking, stirring constantly, until mixture is very thick.

Remove from heat and season with salt and pepper. Beat with an electric beater for 5 minutes, until grits become creamy. Pour into an ungreased 13 x 9 x 2-inch casserole. Chill until set.

Cut the chilled grits into 1½ x 2-inch rectangular pieces. Place them one over another, like rows of fallen dominoes, in a buttered 13 x 9 x 2-inch baking dish that is suitable for serving. Pour ⅓ cup melted butter over the top and sprinkle with grated cheeses. Refrigerate until baking time.

Bake in a preheated 400° oven for 30–35 minutes. For a browner crust, place under the broiler for several minutes.

Gnocchi is an excellent alternative to rice or potatoes and fits in beautifully with tomato dishes and any green vegetable.

55 BARLEY and PINE NUT PILAF

Serves 6

Excellent with game or poultry. Try as a stuffing for game hens or an accompaniment to BUTTERFLIED LEG OF LAMB.

Preparation
25 minutes

Baking
70 minutes

1 cup pearl barley
6 tablespoons butter
2 ounces (⅓ cup) pine nuts
1 cup chopped green onions
½ cup chopped, fresh parsley (2½ tablespoons dried)
¼ teaspoon salt
¼ teaspoon pepper
3⅓ cups chicken broth

Preheat oven to 350°.

Rinse barley in cold water and drain.

In a 10-inch skillet, heat butter and brown pine nuts. Remove with slotted spoon and reserve. Sauté green onions and barley until lightly toasted. Remove from heat. Stir in nuts, parsley, salt, and pepper. Spoon into ungreased 2-quart casserole.

Heat broth to boiling and pour over barley mixture. Stir to blend well. Bake, uncovered, for 1 hour, 10 minutes.

A great "crowd-pleaser", you may prepare ten times this recipe without sacrificing more than a few additional minutes. It is delicious and versatile, complementing the most formal, as well as casual, menus. Try it with CHICKEN BREASTS ALLA MARGHERITA and BRAISED PEAS WITH LETTUCE.

Serves
6 to 8

Preparation
30 minutes

> 5 tablespoons butter
> 1 onion, finely chopped
> 1 cup dry white wine
> 2 cups long grain white rice
> 1 teaspoon salt
> ¼ teaspoon white pepper
> ½ teaspoon saffron threads
> 4–5 cups chicken broth
> 3 tablespoons butter
> 1 cup freshly grated Parmesan cheese

Melt 5 tablespoons of butter in a 4-quart saucepan over moderate heat. Add onion and stir until transparent but do not brown. Add wine and cook over a brisk flame until evaporated.

Add rice, season with salt and white pepper, and stir until every grain is coated with butter. Add saffron and about two cups of chicken broth. Let it almost completely evaporate before adding remaining broth, a little at a time. Reduce heat, continuing to cook, uncovered and stirring frequently, for about 20 to 25 minutes or until it has reached the "al dente" stage (a nutty-like texture). Remove from the fire and add remaining butter plus several tablespoons of the grated cheese.

Place rest of cheese in a serving bowl for those guests who wish extra.

57 WILD RICE in a CASSEROLE

Serves 6 There are so many menus that wild rice complements.

Soaking overnight

Preparation 15 minutes

Baking 40 minutes

1 cup wild rice, soaked overnight
1 10½-ounce can consommé, undiluted
4 tablespoons butter
¾ pound mushrooms, sliced
1½ cups finely chopped celery
1 bunch green onions, sliced
1 6-ounce can water chestnuts, drained and sliced (optional)
½ cup vermouth
Butter

Rinse wild rice well and drain. Combine with consommé in a large sauce pan and simmer, covered, until liquid is absorbed, about 30 minutes.

In a skillet, melt butter and sauté vegetables until limp. Combine with cooked rice and place in a buttered, 2-quart casserole. Refrigerate until ready to use.

When ready to heat, add vermouth and dot with butter. Bake, covered, in 350° oven for 30–40 minutes.

58 MUSHROOM-RICE RING

Serves 6 to 8

Preparation 10 minutes A very attractive, easy way to dress up a dinner party. Surround the rice ring and fill its center with a pretty green vegetable such as Chinese pea pods or broccoli.

1 cup chopped mushrooms
2 tablespoons butter
¼ teaspoon nutmeg
5–6 cups cooked, long-grain white rice

In a medium skillet, sauté the chopped mushrooms in the butter until tender but not brown. Season with nutmeg. Combine mushrooms and rice and turn into a well-buttered, 5 to 6-cup ring mold, pressing mixture down gently. Turn out at once on a warm serving plate or keep the mold warm in a pan of hot water until ready to serve.

Wonderfully delicious but very rich, so be cautious in your menu planning. We suggest grilled meats or simple chicken entrees, accompanied by broiled tomatoes and a green vegetable such as SHREDDED ZUCCHINI.

Serves 8

Preparation 20 minutes

Baking 10 minutes

    2 pounds mushrooms, sliced
    4 tablespoons butter
    ⅔ cup sour cream
    2 tablespoons flour
    ½ teaspoon salt
    ⅛ teaspoon freshly ground pepper
    ½ cup chopped parsley
    1 cup shredded Gruyére or Swiss cheese

Preheat oven to 425°.

Sauté the sliced mushrooms in butter for 1 minute, stirring. Cover the skillet and cook gently until the mushrooms are juicy, about 3–5 minutes.

In a bowl, blend the sour cream, flour, salt, and pepper. Stir gently into the mushrooms and heat to boiling. Remove from the heat immediately. Pour into a shallow, ungreased, 8 x 12-inch casserole. Combine the parsley and shredded cheese and sprinkle on top of the casserole. Bake, uncovered, for 10 minutes.

Except for baking, this dish may be prepared ahead of time.

60 MUSHROOMS FLORENTINE

Serves
4 to 6

Preparation
15 minutes

Baking
20 minutes

These are right in almost any menu and may be prepared as a first course or as a decorative vegetable.

12 large mushrooms, 2½–3 inches in diameter
2 pounds fresh spinach (or 1 10-ounce package frozen)
¼ cup butter
1 medium onion, minced
1 egg yolk
½ teaspoon salt
⅛ teaspoon pepper
⅛ teaspoon freshly ground nutmeg
¼ cup grated Parmesan cheese

Preheat over to 325°.

Clean mushrooms and snap out stems. Finely chop stems and set aside.

Thoroughly wash and drain spinach. Cook the spinach, covered, in just the water that clings to the leaves for 4–5 minutes. Squeeze all water from the spinach and chop finely. If preparing frozen spinach, be sure to drain *very* well.

Melt butter in frying pan over medium heat. Add mushroom caps only to coat with butter, then transfer them to an 8 x 12-inch baking dish. Add the onion and chopped mushroom stems to the frying pan and cook until the onion is limp. Stir in the spinach and remove pan from heat.

Combine the egg yolk, salt, pepper, nutmeg, and 2½ tablespoons of Parmesan cheese and add to spinach mixture. Mound the mixture in the mushroom caps and sprinkle with the remaining cheese. If made ahead, cover and chill up to 24 hours.

Bake, uncovered, for 20 minutes or until heated through and tender.

CELERY with ALMONDS

If you did not like celery before, you will indeed now. This vegetable complements seafood such as SOLE INGE-LISE or HUACHINANGO FRANCESCA.

> 4 cups celery, cut in very thin 3-inch long strips
> 3 tablespoons butter
> 2 tablespoons minced chives
> ½ cup finely chopped scallions, with tops
> ½ small clove garlic, minced
> ½ cup slivered almonds, toasted

Using a heavy skillet, melt butter and add the celery. Cook over low heat for about 3 minutes, stirring constantly. Add the chives, scallions, and garlic. Cook a bit longer, still stirring constantly, but do not overcook. The vegetables should be somewhat crisp when served.

To serve, combine the celery mixture and toasted almonds, reserving a few almonds to sprinkle on the top.

TOMATO PUDDING

Do not let its guise as a provincial dish deter you. You'll love the sweet and sour punch and exciting color.

> 4 cups cubed, white sandwich bread
> 2½ cups tomato sauce
> ½ cup butter
> 1 cup brown sugar
> ½ teaspoon salt
> ½ cup chopped green onions

Cut crusts from bread and discard. Cube or tear each slice into 9–12 pieces until you have 4 cups. Place in the bottom of a buttered, shallow 1½–2 quart baking dish.

Combine the tomato sauce, butter, brown sugar, and salt in a saucepan and heat to boiling. Add the green onions and pour over the bread cubes. Bake for 35 minutes at 375°.

63 TOMATOES filled with GREEN PASTA

Serves 8

*Preparation
25 minutes*

*Baking
8 minutes*

The beautiful colors make this a striking vegetable dish for a buffet. It is also nice as a pasta course or served with steak.

¼ pound spinach egg noodles
8 medium-sized tomatoes
Salt and pepper
1 cup heavy cream
1 cup light cream
½ teaspoon ground thyme
½ teaspoon salt
⅛ teaspoon white pepper
Freshly grated Parmesan cheese

Preheat oven to 350°.

Cook noodles in boiling, salted water, according to package directions, until "al dente", firm to the bite. Drain well.

Cut tops off tomatoes and scoop out insides. (Reserve the flesh for making tomato sauces or adding to soups or omelets.) Season insides of shells with salt and pepper and set aside.

Heat the 2 creams in a medium-sized saucepan. Season with thyme, salt and white pepper. Add the drained noodles and simmer gently until all liquid is absorbed, about 15 minutes, stirring occasionally. Add more salt, if necessary.

Meanwhile, place tomatoes in an ungreased, shallow baking dish and bake 5 minutes or until heated through.

Fill the shells with the noodles and bake 3–4 minutes more. Sprinkle tops with cheese and serve.

A very pretty combination of vegetables for a buffet, large or small.

Serves 8

*Preparation
25 minutes*

*Baking
40 minutes*

> 3 pounds fresh spinach (or 2 10-ounce packages frozen)
> 3 tablespoons butter, melted
> 6 eggs, slightly beaten
> 1 ⅓ cups milk
> 2 medium-sized onions, minced
> 1 ¼–1 ½ teaspoons salt
> ¼ teaspoon pepper
> 1 tablespoon white vinegar
> ¼ teaspoon savory
> 8 tomato slices, ¼-inch thick and slightly wider than molds
> Salt and pepper

Thoroughly wash and drain spinach. Cook spinach, covered, in just the water that clings to the leaves for 4–5 minutes. Squeeze all water from the spinach and chop finely.

In a medium-sized bowl, combine spinach, melted butter, eggs, milk, onions, salt, pepper, vinegar, and savory.

Generously butter 8 5-ounce custard cups or timbale molds. Divide the spinach mixture between the cups. Place the cups in a shallow roasting pan in 1-inch hot water.

Bake 35–40 minutes or until the custard is set. This may be done in the morning and then reheated by covering with foil and setting in hot water in a 350° oven for 10 minutes. Otherwise, you may cover the baking pan with foil and set on back of stove to keep warm until serving.

To serve, sprinkle raw tomato slices with salt and pepper. Loosen the custard from the sides of each mold with a knife. Lay tomato slices over the tops of molds and invert. Set on a serving platter lavished with watercress.

65 SPANISH BEANS

Serves
8 to 10

Soaking
overnight

Preparation
15 minutes

Cooking
3 hours

A blend of pioneer and "south of the border" influences, this recipe has been in the collection of one of our oldest California families for at least four generations. It is at its best cooked and served in a wrought-iron pot.

2 pounds dried cranberry or pinto beans
1 cup olive oil
2 cloves garlic, minced
2 onions, chopped
1 ham hock, quartered by your butcher
2 large tomatoes, peeled and quartered
1 8-ounce can tomato sauce
1 tablespoon chili powder
Salt to taste

Soak beans for several hours or overnight. Drain. Place in a heavy pot and cover with boiling water. Add oil, garlic, onions, and ham hock. Bring to a very slow boil and simmer, uncovered, until soft; about 2 to 3 hours. The beans must be watched and stirred occasionally or they will tend to burn. Add remaining ingredients and simmer for another half-hour or so. Add more salt, if necessary.

Perfect for outdoor barbecues or served with Mexican specialties.

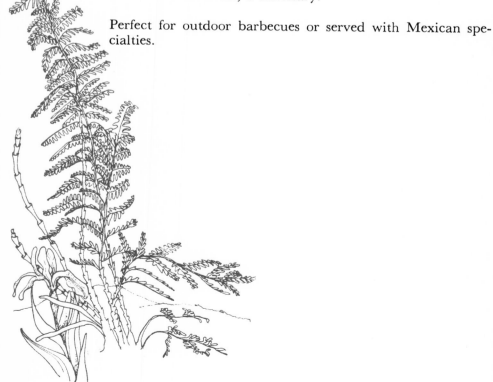

This is a delightfully understated way to serve green beans. They are easily prepared ahead of time, still retaining their crispness and color.

3 pounds fresh green beans, trimmed, washed, and cut
7 quarts boiling water in a large kettle
3½ tablespoons salt

6–8 tablespoons softened butter, cut in 4 pieces
Salt and freshly ground pepper to taste
1 tablespoon lemon juice
3 tablespoons minced parsley

To blanch beans, drop a handful at a time into the boiling, salted water. Bring water back to a boil as quickly as possible, reduce heat and boil beans slowly, uncovered. After 7 minutes, test the beans frequently by biting into one each time.

When they are tender but still slightly crunchy, drain immediately. Run cold water over beans 3–4 minutes, then drain. These latter steps are very important. If preparing ahead, at this point refrigerate the beans in plastic bags until ready to finish cooking.

Toss the beans in a large, heavy skillet over moderately high heat to evaporate moisture and reheat them. Toss briefly with a piece of butter and salt and pepper to taste. Add rest of butter gradually, alternating with drops of lemon juice while still tossing.

Taste for seasoning. Turn into a hot vegetable dish. Sprinkle with parsley and serve immediately.

You may easily reduce the quantities of this recipe, respectively.

67 ONIONS filled with BROCCOLI

Serves 6

Preparation
30 minutes

Baking
20 minutes

Eye-appeal and unusual presentations are important factors in successful menus. This vegetable dish is unique and yet a nice combination of popular flavors. Serve it with CARROTS IN MINT SAUCE or TOMATO PUDDING, and veal, beef, or lamb entrees.

3 medium-large Spanish (sweet) onions, peeled
1 pound fresh broccoli
½ cup grated Parmesan cheese
⅓ cup mayonnaise
2 teaspoons lemon juice

Preheat oven 375°.

Cut the onions in half crosswise. Gently parboil them in salted water for 10–12 minutes. Drain. Remove their centers, leaving ¾-inch walls. Do not be concerned if some of the onions come apart in cooking. They can easily be reassembled. Chop the center portions to equal 1 cup.

Cook the broccoli in boiling salted water until just tender. Chop the tender tops. Reserve the stems for another use. Combine the chopped broccoli with the chopped onion, Parmesan cheese, mayonnaise, and lemon juice.

Mound the broccoli mixture in the onion halves. Bake in a buttered, 9 to 10-inch pie plate or shallow casserole, uncovered, for 20 minutes.

Except for the baking process, these may be prepared early in the day.

A delightful, oriental touch to serving a vegetable. Because the broccoli stems are peeled, there is very little wasted and just the right amount of crispness.

Serves
6 to 8

Preparation
15 minutes

Cooking
4–7 minutes

    3 pounds broccoli
    1 cup chicken broth
    2 teaspoons cornstarch
    2 teaspoons soy sauce
    ½ teaspoon monosodium glutamate (optional)
    Pinch of ginger
    Salt to taste
    ¼ cup peanut oil

Wash broccoli. Remove flowers, separating into bite-sized pieces. Cut 1 to 2 inches from base of stems, depending on toughness, and discard. Remove leaves from remaining stems and peel. Slice diagonally, between ⅛ to ¼ inch thick. Unusually large slices should be cut in halves or quarters.

Combine remaining ingredients except oil and set aside. Heat oil in a heavy skillet or wok until very hot. Add stems and toss or stir for 1 minute. Add flowers and continue tossing for another minute. Push broccoli to sides of pan and pour chicken broth mixture into center. Cook slowly until this thickens then mix broccoli back into sauce. Cover and cook slowly for 2 to 3 minutes. If you wish broccoli to be a little more tender, stir and toss another 2 minutes. Serve immediately.

This is nice in almost any menu.

69 SHREDDED ZUCCHINI

Serves 6 Zucchini becomes elegant!

Preparation
10 minutes

6 small zucchini
2 tablespoons butter
6 green onions, chopped
Salt and freshly ground pepper to taste
Freshly ground nutmeg
Parmesan cheese (optional)

Shred zucchini. (A food processor is ideal, using the coarser shredding disk.) Drain on paper towels for a few minutes.

Place zucchini in a large saucepan or skillet with butter and green onions. Turn on high heat and toss zucchini mixture until just heated through. Remove from heat and season to taste with salt, pepper, and freshly ground nutmeg. Serve immediately, sprinkling with Parmesan cheese if you wish.

70 BRAISED PEAS with LETTUCE

Serves 4 You will like this different approach to the French method of cooking peas. If fresh peas are not available in the market, you
Preparation
10 minutes may use 2 10-ounce packages of frozen petite peas.

Cooking
10 minutes

2 cups shredded lettuce
2 cups shelled green peas (2 pounds unshelled)
¼ cup sliced scallions
1 teaspoon sugar
¼ teaspoon salt
¼ teaspoon crushed, dried summer savory (¾ teaspoon fresh)
⅛ teaspoon white pepper
2 tablespoons butter, cut up

Place 1 cup shredded lettuce in a large saucepan. Top with the peas and scallions. Sprinkle with sugar, salt, savory, and white pepper. Dot with butter and top with the remaining lettuce.

Cover tightly and cook over medium-low heat for 5–10 minutes, until the peas are tender.

The leek's delicate flavor belies that it is an onion. Known in Europe as "the poor man's asparagus", it has enjoyed just the opposite reputation in this country. Until recently, leeks were scarce and always expensive. Much to our delight, California's growers have changed that fact.

Serves 6

Preparation
30 minutes

Cooking
25 minutes

Baking
20 minutes

 8 large leeks
 8 slices of bacon, cut in 2-inch pieces
 1 cup water
 Salt and pepper to taste
 Dash of ground thyme
 2 tablespoons butter
 2 tablespoons flour
 1 cup milk
 1 egg yolk
 ½ cup heavy cream
 2 tablespoons grated Swiss cheese

Preheat oven to 375°.

Trim off root ends of leeks. Cut off tops, leaving 1–2 inches of light green. Cut the stalks in half lengthwise and wash thoroughly under running water, holding leaves apart. Again, cut in half lengthwise, then into 2-inch pieces.

Brown bacon in a skillet. Drain fat. Add leeks, water, salt, pepper, and thyme. Cover tightly and cook until leeks are tender and water has evaporated, about 20–25 minutes.

Melt the butter in a saucepan and stir in flour with a whisk until smooth. Add milk, stirring and cooking until it comes to a boil. Cook 5 minutes. Stir the egg yolk and cream together and mix into the white sauce. Combine the sauce and leeks.

Pour all into a lightly buttered, 9 to 10-inch pie plate or shallow casserole. Sprinkle with the cheese and bake 20 minutes or until golden.

72 CARROT SOUFFLÉ

Serves 8

Preparation 30 minutes

Baking 1 hour

Different, delicious, and never falls! Your guests who cannot abide carrots will ask for the recipe.

> 2 cups cooked and pureed carrots*
> 2 teaspoons lemon juice
> 2 tablespoons minced or grated onion
> ½ cup butter, softened
> ¼ cup sugar
> 1 tablespoon flour
> 1 teaspoon salt
> ¼ teaspoon cinnamon
> 1 cup milk
> 3 eggs

Preheat oven to 350°.

*Carrots may be cooked and pureed hours ahead of time, adding the lemon juice and covering tightly until ready to mix.

Beat all ingredients together until smooth. Pour into a 2-quart, lightly buttered soufflé dish or casserole. Bake, uncovered, for 45 minutes to 1 hour until center is firm to touch.

There is a sweetness to this recipe that dictates the choice of menu. It is lovely with ROAST VEAL DIJON and fresh, young asparagus.

Lovely with veal, lamb, and poultry, they lend that perfect touch of color. The lemon is the taste secret! If you wish, prepare the carrots and sauce well-ahead of time, but do not combine until ready to serve.

Serves 4

Preparation
15 minutes

> 6 carrots, diced, sliced, or slivered
> ⅓ cup reserved liquid
> 2 tablespoons butter
> 1 tablespoon sugar
> 1 teaspoon cornstarch
> ⅛ teaspoon salt
> Juice and grated rind of a lemon half
> 1 tablespoon finely chopped mint leaves

Parboil carrots, covered, in a small amount of boiling, salted water for 4–8 minutes, depending upon thickness and age of carrots. Cook until barely tender. Drain, reserving ⅓ cup of the liquid.

Melt butter in a medium saucepan. Combine sugar, cornstarch, and salt, and stir into butter. Add remaining ingredients and reserved liquid. Stir until just thickened.

When ready to serve, add carrots to heated sauce and toss to glaze.

74 APRICOT or PEACH CHUTNEY

Yield
3–5 pints

Preparation
45 minutes

Cooking
1¼ hours

The luscious colors in sparkling jars are decorative in any pantry and one has such a nice feeling of accomplishment!

1¼ cups cider vinegar
1¾ cups sugar
2½ pounds ripe apricots or peaches
2 oranges
1 lemon
3 medium white onions
6 sweet red peppers or pimento
1 cup seedless raisins
4 ounces candied ginger, chopped
1 clove garlic, minced
1 teaspoon salt
¾ cup slivered almonds
½ cup cider vinegar
1 teaspoon ground ginger

In a heavy 4 to 5-quart pan, gently boil the vinegar and sugar for 5 minutes.

Wash, pit, and chop the unpeeled apricots or peaches. You may use a meat grinder or food processor, if you wish. It is a matter of taste as to the size of the pieces. Add the fruit to the pan and simmer 10 minutes, uncovered.

Seed but do not peel oranges and lemon. Finely chop them and the onions, and add to pan. Seed and chop the peppers in larger pieces for color effect. Add to pan with raisins, candied ginger, garlic, and salt. Simmer 30 minutes, uncovered.

Add the almonds, remaining vinegar, and ground ginger to the pan and simmer, uncovered, another 30 minutes to reduce the liquid. Stir frequently to prevent sticking. Ladle immediately into sterile jars and seal carefully.

A welcome gift at any time, it is a delicious relish with meat, poultry, and especially with curries. Once opened, it should be refrigerated but will keep several months.

The color and flavors make this a unique accompaniment for almost any entree . . . chicken, beef, pork, lamb.

Serves 8

Preparation
10 minutes

4 firm-ripe papayas
8 tablespoons butter
4 tablespoons lime juice
1 teaspoon ground ginger
8 thin slices of lime
Dash of cayenne

Baking
30 minutes

Preheat oven to 350°.

Cut papayas in half, lengthwise, and scoop out seeds. Arrange in a glass baking dish with ⅛-inch warm water in bottom.

In each papaya hollow, place 1 tablespoon butter, ½ tablespoon lime juice and ⅛ teaspoon ground ginger.

Bake for 30 minutes, basting 10 minutes before done. Place a slice of lime at edge of each papaya half. Add a dash of cayenne and serve warm.

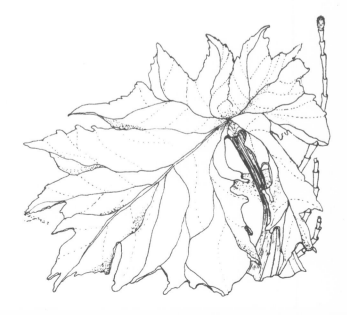

Serves
8 to 10

Preparation
15 minutes

Chill
2–3 hours

As you well-know, the secret to a great salad is crisp, cold greens. This method insures it.

6 tablespoons olive oil
2 tablespoons white wine vinegar with tarragon
½ teaspoon salt
1 small clove garlic, minced
1 small head Boston lettuce
2 heads butter or Bibb lettuce
3 stalks Belgian endive
½ bunch watercress
2 tablespoons chopped parsley
2 tablespoons chopped chives
1 tablespoon chopped fresh dill (1 teaspoon dried)
2 teaspoons chopped fresh thyme leaves (½ teaspoon dried)
1 medium avocado

Combine the olive oil, vinegar, salt, and garlic in bottom of your salad bowl.

Wash lettuce leaves and dry *very* well. Tear into bite-sized pieces over dressing. *Do not toss.* Wash endive, dry, and slice over lettuce. Wash watercress and discard stems. Add to lettuce. Sprinkle parsley, chives, dill, and thyme over top of leaves. Cover bowl tightly with plastic wrap and chill in refrigerator several hours.

Just before serving, peel and slice avocado and add to greens. Toss all gently but well.

You'll enjoy the touch of curry. Keep the salad simple when featuring with delicate entrees such as SALMON MOUSSE or in a dinner menu ... men definitely prefer it that way! Let fancy take over, though, for a brunch or luncheon and use any or all of the suggested garnishes.

Serves 6 to 8

Preparation 15 minutes

Chill

2 tablespoons white wine vinegar
1 tablespoon vermouth
2 teaspoons Dijon mustard
1 teaspoon soy sauce
½ teaspoon curry powder
½ teaspoon sugar
½ teaspoon salt
¼ teaspoon freshly ground pepper
⅓ cup salad oil
1–1¼ pounds spinach

Combine all of the ingredients except the spinach in a jar and shake well. Pour into salad bowl.

Wash and dry spinach. Remove any tough stems. Tear leaves into bite-sized pieces and place in salad bowl on top of dressing. *Do not toss.* Cover bowl tightly with plastic wrap and refrigerate. Toss well just before serving, including any or all of the following garnishes, if you wish.

1 green apple, diced
⅓ cup dry-roasted Spanish peanuts
¼ cup golden raisins
1 bunch scallions, thinly sliced
1 tablespoon sesame seeds, toasted

Unadorned, its an excellent dinner salad with lamb or chicken. For luncheon, we suggest serving the garnished version with AVOCADO CRAB MORNAY.

78 WINTER SALAD

Serves 6

*Preparation
20 minutes*

This salad has beautiful colors and is an excellent substitute for the seemingly omnipresent tossed green salad.

> 3 tablespoons finely chopped parsley
> ¼ cup olive oil
> ¼ cup salad oil
> 1 tablespoon white vinegar
> 1 tablespoon lemon juice
> 1 teaspoon Dijon wine mustard
> ½ teaspoon salt
> ⅛ teaspoon freshly ground pepper
> ½ pound mushrooms
> 12 radishes
> ¼ jícama, peeled*
> 4–6 green onions, thinly sliced by hand
> 1 clove garlic, minced
> Lettuce

Combine the parsley, oils, vinegar, lemon juice, mustard, salt, and pepper in a jar and shake well.

Thinly slice the mushrooms, radishes, and jícama. If not using immediately, refrigerate the vegetables in separate containers covered with plastic wrap. When ready to serve, combine with the onions, garlic, and dressing, and serve in lettuce cups.

Note: The parsley and dressing ingredients may be prepared in a food processor, as well as the mushrooms, radishes, and jícama. For a more refined appearance, we suggest that the onions be sliced by hand.

*Jícama is a mild, turnip-like tuber from Mexico and South America that is becoming increasingly popular in this country. If you cannot locate one, you may substitute turnip.

Unique and delicious! Serve at picnics and tailgate parties with an abundance of butter lettuce leaves heaped in a napkin-lined basket. Instruct your guests to place a spoonful of the salad on a lettuce leaf, then roll up to eat as a sandwich.

*Serves
6 to 8*

*Soaking
overnight*

1 cup wild rice
1¼ cups chicken broth
1 clove garlic
1 bunch scallions, chopped
3 tablespoons butter
1 cup chopped mushrooms (½ pound)
3 strips lean bacon, diced, and fried crisp
½ cup chopped green olives with pimento
⅓ cup olive oil
3 tablespoons white wine vinegar with tarragon*
½ teaspoon dried marjoram
Salt and freshly ground pepper to taste

*Preparation
15 minutes*

*Cooking
25 minutes*

*Marinate
24 hours*

Soak rice in cold water overnight. Rinse then simmer, covered, in chicken broth with garlic until all liquid is absorbed, about 25–30 minutes. Rice should be dry yet fluffy. Discard garlic.

In a medium-sized skillet, sauté the scallions until soft. Add mushrooms and toss briefly over high heat. Add to the rice along with remaining ingredients. Toss well, taste for salt and pepper, and chill, preferably 24 hours. Serve cold, tossing once more.

*Note: In place of tarragon vinegar, you may substitute 3 tablespoons lemon juice and 1 teaspoon tarragon. Also, this recipe is attractive served in tomato shells.

80 MAISON JAUSSAUD'S BEANS

Serves 24

*Preparation
30 minutes*

*Cooking
2 hours*

*Marinate
8 hours*

Far more than just a bean salad, this is an excellent version of one made for many years by the matriarch of a French family in southern California and served in their popular restaurant, "Maison Jaussaud". It is an ideal dish for picnics and tailgate parties or as an appetizer with thin slices of fresh French bread and pickled beef tongue.

2 pounds small, white navy beans
2 cups olive oil
1¼ cups lemon juice
½ cup white vinegar
3 cups finely chopped celery
½ cup plus 1 tablespoon finely chopped green
   bell pepper
½ cup chopped parsley
2 tablespoons finely chopped onion
4½ teaspoons salt
¼ teaspoon thyme

Soak and cook beans according to package directions but do not overcook. They should retain their shape.

Marinate in the remaining ingredients, tightly covered, 8 hours or more, stirring occasionally.

You do not have to be a "baker" to make this fabulous bread.

2 cups lukewarm water
1 package dry yeast
1 tablespoon sugar
2 teaspoons salt
4 cups bread flour (but all-purpose will do)
1 tablespoon cornmeal
Melted butter

In a large bowl, combine the water, yeast, sugar, and salt. Stir until dissolved. Stir in bread flour. Turn the dough out onto a floured plate.

Clean the bowl and grease with butter. Return the dough to the bowl and cover with a damp towel. Let rise in a warm place for 45 minutes or until double in bulk.

Grease a baking sheet and sprinkle it with 1 tablespoon of cornmeal. Flour your hands and divide the dough into 2 parts, shaping each into an oblong loaf but do not knead. Place both loaves on the prepared baking sheet. Let the loaves rise another 45 minutes until almost doubled.

Preheat oven to 425°.

Brush the tops of the loaves with melted butter and bake 10 minutes. Reduce the temperature to 375° and bake 20 minutes more.

While the loaves are still hot, brush with more butter and serve. You will love the feeling of triumph!

Serves
6 to 8

Yield
Two loaves

Preparation
15 minutes

Rising
1½ hours

Baking
30 minutes

82 PARTY ROLLS

Yield
3 dozen

These are far more delicious than their commercial counter-parts and so easy to make.

Preparation
20 minutes

½ cup butter, softened
½ cup vegetable shortening
1 cup sugar

Refrigeration
4–8 hours

1½ teaspoons salt
1 cup boiling water
2 packages dry yeast

Rising
3 hours

2 eggs, beaten
1 cup cold water
6 cups all-purpose flour, unsifted

Baking
15 minutes

Dissolve butter, shortening, sugar, and salt in boiling water. Cool.

Dissolve yeast in cooled mixture. Add eggs, cold water, and flour. Stir just to mix and place in refrigerator for at least 4 hours or overnight.

Three hours before use, roll into 3 circles but do not knead. Cut each circle into 12 segments as for a pie. Starting at wide end, roll up each segment and place, tip down, on an un-greased baking sheet, far enough apart so that they will not touch during rising or baking. Let rise in a moderately warm place for 3 hours.

Preheat oven to 400°. Bake 12–15 minutes until golden brown.

Gougère is a breeze-of-a-method for making pastry that origi-
nated many, many years ago in France. Rather like a glorified
cream puff or pop-over, it is beautiful with soups, salads, and
delicate stews such as WATERZOOIE VAN KIP or ARNI AV-
GOLEMENO.

Serves
6 to 8

Preparation
10 minutes

Baking
45 minutes

   1 cup milk
   ¼ cup butter, cut in pieces
   ½ teaspoon salt
   Dash of pepper
   1 cup all-purpose flour, unsifted
   4 eggs
   1 cup shredded Swiss cheese

Preheat oven to 375°.

In a heavy, 2-quart saucepan, heat the milk, butter, salt, and
pepper, bringing to a full boil. Add the flour all at once,
stirring constantly with a wooden spatula or spoon. Almost
immediately the dough will leave the sides of the pan and
form a ball. Remove from heat.

With the wooden spatula, beat the eggs into the dough, one at
a time, until the mixture is smooth and well-blended. Stir in
half of the cheese. Do not be concerned about the sticky consistency of the dough.

Using three-fourths of the dough, place 8 spoonfuls in a circle
on an ungreased baking sheet. The mounds should barely
touch each other, forming a circle about 8 inches in diameter
with a 2-inch space in the center. With rest of dough, place a
smaller mound on top of each larger one. Sprinkle remaining
½ cup of cheese over all.

Bake for 45 minutes or until puffs are lightly browned and
crisp. Try not to open the oven door for the first 40 minutes
of baking. Serve immediately.

84 SESAME THINS and RYE MELBAS

Yield
72 wafers

Preparation
15 minutes

Baking
20 minutes

Both of these are delectable additions to soup or salad courses. They store well for a week or two in tightly covered tins or may be frozen.

SESAME THINS

1 1-pound loaf of flavorful white bread, sliced extra thin
1 cup butter, softened
4 ounces sesame seeds

Preheat oven to 250°–275°.

Spread 1 side of each slice of bread generously with softened butter. Remove crusts and cut each slice into 3 fingers. Place the fingers against each other on an ungreased baking sheet. Sprinkle lavishly with sesame seeds and bake until golden brown, about 20–30 minutes.

RYE MELBAS

1 long, thin loaf of rye bread, unsliced
Butter, softened

Freeze bread. Ask your butcher or deli to slice the frozen bread paper-thin, or use an electric knife.

Spread each slice *very* lightly with softened butter. Place on ungreased baking sheets and bake at 250°–275° for 20–30 minutes or until crisp.

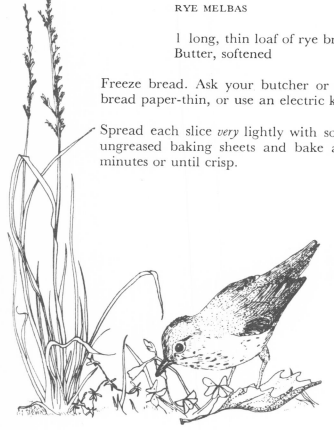

This is an absolute must with THE CHICKEN SALADS. The best banana bread that we have tasted, it stays moist indefinitely... although it is always gone before we can prove that fact!

Yield
Two loaves

Preparation
20 minutes

2 cups granulated sugar
1 cup softened butter
6 ripe bananas, mashed (approximately 3 cups)
4 eggs, well-beaten
2½ cups cake flour
2 teaspoons baking soda
1 teaspoon salt

Baking
45–60 minutes

Preheat oven to 350°.

With electric beater, cream together sugar and butter until light and fluffy. Add bananas and eggs, beating until well-mixed.

Sift together dry ingredients three times. Blend with banana mixture but *do not* overmix.

Pour into 2 lightly-greased loaf pans. Bake for 45 minutes to one hour, until firm in the centers and the edges begin to separate from pans.

Cool on a rack for 10 minutes before removing from pans. These freeze beautifully.

86 PINEAPPLE ICE

Serves 6

What fun this is to make and serve! A food processor is a must, though.

Preparation
15 minutes

1 large, ripe, pretty pineapple
¼–½ cup sugar
2 tablespoons lemon juice

Freeze
3 hours

Cut the top from the pineapple and reserve in the refrigerator. With a long, thin, sharp knife, carefully cut around inside of shell, about ½-inch from edge. To loosen pulp from bottom of shell, while maintaining as small an opening as possible, insert your knife ½-inch above bottom of pineapple and carefully work blade around in a semi-circle. Remove knife, turn it over, and repeat for remaining half-circle. The pulp should lift out easily.

Discard the hard core and place the pulp in the food processor. Scrape the inside walls and bottom of the pineapple with a large spoon until smooth, placing any additional fruit in the processor. Depending on size and sweetness of pineapple, add ¼–½ cup sugar and lemon juice. Puree the mixture then pour into a shallow container and place in freezer along with shell.

When puree is frozen to a slushy consistency, about 1 hour, respin in processor until smooth and creamy. Pour into frozen shell and refreeze at least 2 hours.

To serve, place the pineapple and its top in a pretty glass dish or a bed of mint sprigs and let your guests help themselves. CHOCOLATE MACAROONS are a nice extra touch.

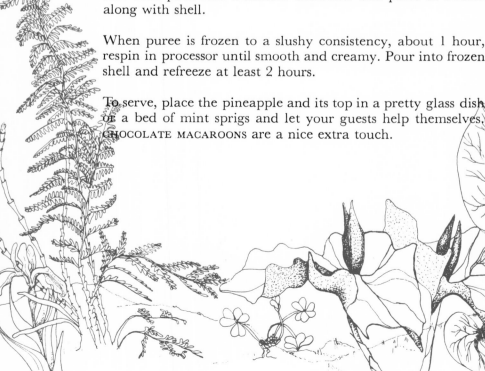

LEMON SNOW with GRAND MARNIER SAUCE 87

A delightfully sophisticated version of an old-fashioned dessert.

2/3 cup sugar
1 envelope unflavored gelatin
1½ cups boiling water
⅓ cup fresh lemon juice
¼ teaspoon finely grated lemon peel
3 egg whites

Combine the sugar and gelatin in a large bowl. Add boiling water, stirring until gelatin is dissolved. Stir in lemon juice and peel.

Chill the mixture until it becomes syrupy. This can be done more quickly if the bowl is set within a larger bowl that has been partially filled with ice.

Beat the egg whites until stiff. Add to the syrupy mixture, beating until it begins to thicken slightly, about 5 minutes. Pour into a pretty serving dish and chill at least 2 hours, until set.

3 egg yolks
¼ cup sugar
⅓ cup butter, melted
3 tablespoons fresh lemon juice
3 tablespoons Grand Marnier
½ cup heavy cream
1 teaspoon finely grated lemon peel

Beat egg yolks until thick and light-colored. Gradually beat in sugar and then butter, lemon juice, and Grand Marnier.

Beat cream until thick and glossy but not stiff. Fold into egg mixture along with the lemon peel. Chill thoroughly.

To serve, decorate LEMON SNOW with mint leaves, if you wish, and pass with GRAND MARNIER SAUCE in a separate bowl.

88 SUMMER LEMON SOUFFLÉ

Serves 8

Preparation
15 minutes

Freeze
6 hours

A delicious, refreshing dessert.

1 envelope unflavored gelatin
¼ cup cold water
6 egg yolks
1 cup sugar
⅔ cup lemon juice
Grated rind of 2 lemons
4 egg whites
1½ cups heavy cream
Lemon slices
Whipped cream

Tear off a piece of waxed paper long enough to surround a 1-quart soufflé dish*. Fold paper in half lengthwise and brush one side with vegetable oil. Tie the paper around the soufflé dish with the oiled side turned inward and extending 2 inches above the rim.

Soften gelatin in the cold water. In a non-aluminum saucepan, beat egg yolks and sugar until thick and light. Stir in lemon juice and cook over low heat, beating steadily until thickened and hot, but not boiling. Mix in gelatin until dissolved and then lemon rind. Remove from heat and cool to room temperature, stirring occasionally.

Beat the 4 egg whites until stiff but not dry. Fold into the cooled lemon mixture. Whip the cream and fold in. Slowly pour into the soufflé dish. The mixture should rise above the rim. Freeze and serve frozen.

When ready to serve, remove collar and decorate the top with paper-thin lemon slices and additional whipped cream. A bowl of fresh blueberries is a pretty complement.

Note: This recipe may be made in a 9-inch springform pan without using a collar, then unmolded when served. It should not be left in a metal pan more than 24 hours.

It is lovely, pleasing to any palate any time of the year.

Serves 8

1 envelope unflavored gelatin
2 tablespoons cold water
1 10½–ounce package frozen raspberries, defrosted
¾ cup sugar
1 cup egg whites (approximately 7–8 eggs)
1 cup heavy cream

Preparation
15 minutes

Chill

Tear off a piece of waxed paper long enough to surround a 1-quart soufflé dish. Fold paper in half lengthwise and brush one side with vegetable oil. With oiled side turned inward, tie the paper around the soufflé dish, extending it 2 inches above the rim.

In a medium, stainless steel saucepan, soften gelatin in water. Puree, then strain berries through a sieve. Add pureed berries to gelatin with the sugar and heat, stirring, until the gelatin and sugar have dissolved. Transfer to a large bowl and chill until cool but not yet gelled.

Beat whites until stiff and fold into berries. Whip the cream and fold into berry mixture.

Spoon carefully into the soufflé dish. The mixture should rise above the rim. Chill overnight or freeze until several hours before serving. When ready to serve, remove collar and accompany with the following sauce:

1 10½–ounce package frozen raspberries, defrosted
¼ cup sugar
2 tablespoons framboise (raspberry liquor)

Puree and strain berries. Combine with sugar and framboise.

90 ROYAL MERINGUE

Serves 8

*Preparation
30 minutes*

*Baking
45 minutes*

Cool

A dainty meringue and strawberry confection, it really is fit for royalty and yet wonderfully easy to prepare. You may make it hours ahead of time and, if you have a large mold, you may double the recipe, but increase the baking time accordingly.

8 egg whites
½ teaspoon cream of tartar
1 cup sugar
1½ cups flaked coconut
2 teaspoons almond flavoring
1 10½-ounce package frozen, sliced strawberries, defrosted
1 cup heavy cream
1 pint fresh strawberries, washed and hulled
Sugar
Sprigs of mint (optional)

Whip egg whites and cream of tartar until foamy. Add sugar, 2 tablespoons at a time, beating after each addition. When meringue stands in stiff, glossy peaks, spoon into an ungreased, 10-cup ring mold. Do this carefully to eliminate any large air bubbles.

Set the mold in a shallow roasting pan filled with 1 inch of warm water. Bake 45 minutes at 250° until meringue is set. Cool mold on a rack until the meringue settles. The meringue may remain in its mold all day at room temperature.

Toast coconut until golden brown in a 350° oven, stirring occasionally with a fork. Toss with almond flavoring.

Puree thawed berries in a blender. Beat cream until very thick but shiny. Fold into puree. Chill.

To serve, loosen meringue from mold with a knife that has been dipped in water to prevent tearing. Invert on serving plate and place a bowl of the strawberry cream in the center. Sprinkle the fresh berries with sugar to taste and scatter over the meringue. Sprinkle the toasted coconut over the sauce, berries, and meringue. Garnish with sprigs of mint.

A simple but most pleasing summer treat. Do notice the nice variations.

Serves 4

*Preparation
15 minutes*

*Cool
1 hour*

   1 pint strawberries
   1 tablespoon sugar
   ½ cup sugar
   2 teaspoons grated orange rind
   ½ cup orange juice
   1 cup heavy cream

Wash and hull berries, cutting in half or leaving whole. Combine them with 1 tablespoon sugar in a small bowl.

Combine the ½ cup sugar, orange rind, and orange juice in a small saucepan. Bring to a boil, stirring only until the sugar dissolves. Simmer 10 minutes without stirring. Cool completely.

Whip cream until soft peaks form. Gently fold in orange syrup. Serve over berries.

Variations: Substitute fresh blueberries or raspberries and, instead of orange, use lemon juice and rind in the same quantities.

Serves 6 The peaches retain their gorgeous blush.

Preparation
40 minutes

Chill

2½ cups water
1½ cups sugar
1 vanilla bean, split lengthwise
6 large, ripe peaches, unpeeled
½ cup brandy
Sprigs of mint (optional)

In a large enamel or stainless steel saucepan, combine water, sugar, and vanilla bean. Dissolve sugar over moderate heat, brushing down crystals that may cling to the sides of the pan with a brush dipped in cold water. Bring syrup to a boil, lower heat, and simmer for 10 minutes without stirring.

Add the whole peaches to the syrup and gently simmer, uncovered, for 12–15 minutes, or until barely tender. Cool in the syrup then remove peaches with a slotted spoon.

Add brandy to syrup and cook 5 minutes. Transfer syrup to a bowl. Peel the peaches and add them to syrup. Chill.

Serve the peaches in sherbet glasses with a little of the syrup and sprigs of fresh mint. Pass a sauceboat of warm VANILLA SAUCE.

Yield
2 cups

Preparation
10 minutes

⅔ cup confectioners' sugar
½ cup butter
1 cup heavy cream
1 tablespoon vanilla

In a small saucepan, combine sugar and butter and cook over low heat, stirring until smooth and thick. Remove from heat.

Whip cream into soft peaks. With a whisk, combine with warm butter and sugar mixture. Add vanilla.

Simplicity is an essence of elegance, portrayed so well by this lovely autumn dessert.

Serves 6

*Preparation
45 minutes*

> 5 or 6 cooking apples
> 1 tablespoon butter
> ¼ cup sugar
> ½ stick of cinnamon
> 3 tablespoons chopped walnuts
> 6 firm pears
> 5 ounces red wine
> 1 cup sugar
> ¼ stick of cinnamon
> 1 strip of lemon peel
> 2 ounces cognac or rum

Peel, core, and mince apples. In a skillet, cook the apples in the butter with ¼ cup sugar and a half cinnamon stick. When the apples are soft, discard the cinnamon stick and add the walnuts. Remove from the heat.

Peel the pears. Leave stems attached, if possible.

In a large sauce pan, bring the wine and remaining 1 cup of sugar to a gentle boil and add the quarter stick of cinnamon and lemon peel. Poach the whole pears in the wine syrup until tender.

Place the apple mixture in a serving dish. With a slotted spoon, carefully remove the pears from their syrup and arrange on top of the apples.

Cook the syrup until reduced to half its original amount. Remove cinnamon stick and lemon peel. Pour over pears.

Just before serving, warm the cognac or rum, pour over all, and ignite at the table. (These are also good cold!)

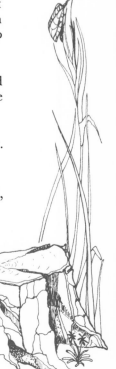

94 PERSIMMON STEAMED PUDDING

Serves
8 to 10

Preparation
20 minutes

Steaming
2 hours

Persimmons are truly a western treat. The bright globes of color on sparse branches give a lift to the often cold, dreary days of November and December. There are many versions of Persimmon Pudding, and there is a school for the ones with raisins and nuts and a school for those without. This recipe represents the latter but is loved by all. It is mystifying that samplers often think it is chocolate. The pudding is dramatic at Christmas-time, served flaming on a silver platter surrounded with holly.

> 1 cup persimmon pulp (3 average persimmons)
> ½ cup butter, softened
> ¾ cup sugar
> 1 beaten egg
> 1 cup sifted flour
> 1¾ teaspoons baking soda
> 1 teaspoon cinnamon
> ¼ teaspoon salt
> ½ cup milk
> 1 teaspoon vanilla

Remove stems from very ripe persimmons and puree, skins and all, in blender to make 1 cup. (Persimmons are ripe enough when insides are like jelly.)

Cream butter and sugar until light and fluffy. Add beaten egg. Sift flour with soda, cinnamon, and salt. Add to butter mixture, alternating with milk. Stir in persimmon pulp and vanilla. Mix well.

Pour batter into a well-greased, 1-quart mold (a 1-pound coffee can will do) and cover tightly with a lid or foil.

Use a kettle or roasting pan that is deeper than mold. Place a rack in the bottom to support mold, and fill with enough warm water so as not to evaporate during steaming, usually about one-fourth of the depth.

Cover kettle tightly and steam on top of stove or in 325° oven for two hours, letting water just simmer. Cool pudding until lukewarm and unmold. If you wish to serve flaming, warm ¼ cup brandy, pour over pudding and light. Pass separately a bowl of sweetened, whipped cream or FOAMY HARD SAUCE.

If making ahead, cool, unmold, and wrap pudding well for storage in refrigerator or freezer. It will keep in your refrigerator for as long as two weeks. To serve, wrap snuggly in foil and re-steam, without water touching foil, until heated through.

This makes a lovely Christmas gift, gaily wrapped in a sheet of green cellophane and tied with red ribbon and holly.

FOAMY HARD SAUCE 95

Delightful over gingerbread or PERSIMMON STEAMED PUDDING.

Yield
3 cups

Preparation
15 minutes

1 cup sugar
½ cup butter, softened
4 egg yolks, beaten
2 ounces sherry or brandy
Pinch of salt
1 cup heavy cream

In top of double boiler, with a whisk or electric beater, cream together sugar and butter. When light, add beaten yolks, brandy, and salt, beating well.

Heat cream until hot but do not boil. Add slowly to rest of ingredients, continuing to beat well.

Place over boiling water, stirring with a whisk until the sauce is the thickness of cream but do not allow it to boil.

This stores well in the refrigerator and may be carefully reheated over warm water.

96 FROZEN MOCHA MOUSSE

Serves 16–20

*Preparation
20 minutes*

A fabulous dessert for large parties, it is divinely rich in chocolate.

> 1 pound semi-sweet baking chocolate
> 3 tablespoons instant coffee granules
> ½ cup boiling water
> 6 egg yolks
> ½ cup sugar
> 1 teaspoon vanilla
> 6 egg whites
> 1½ cups heavy cream, whipped
> ½ cup heavy cream
> Chocolate curls

Melt chocolate over hot water. Dissolve coffee granules in boiling water and cool slightly.

In a medium-sized bowl, beat egg yolks at high speed until foamy. Gradually beat in sugar and continue beating until mixture is very thick and pale yellow. Reduce speed and beat in vanilla, coffee, and melted chocolate.

With clean beaters, beat egg whites in a large mixing bowl until they hold stiff peaks. Stir 1 cup of the beaten whites into chocolate mixture, then stir chocolate mixture into the remaining whites. Gently, but thoroughly, fold in 1½ cups whipped cream. Pour into an 8-inch springform pan and freeze. It will keep nicely in your freezer up to 1 month.

To serve, remove the mousse from the freezer 20–25 minutes before dessert-time and remove springform sides. Whip ½ cup heavy cream and mound on top of mousse, garnishing with chocolate curls.

Note: A nice variation is to line a 9-inch springform pan with 24 Lady Fingers, split and brushed with ¼ cup light rum, overlapping bottom pieces to fit. Fill with MOCHA MOUSSE and freeze. Voila! MOCHA CHARLOTTE!

PETITS POTS of CHOCOLATE

When happily replete, your guests will love this charming dessert served in the living room with steaming demitasse.

Serves 8

*Preparation
15 minutes*

*Chill
2 hours*

    4 ounces semi-sweet chocolate
    2 tablespoons butter
Juice of 1 orange
    1 tablespoon Grand Marnier
    4 egg yolks, beaten
    3 egg whites

Melt chocolate with butter and orange juice in the top of a double boiler. Remove from heat and stir in Grand Marnier. Cool slightly. Add beaten egg yolks to chocolate mixture and mix well. Beat egg whites until stiff but not dry. Gently fold into chocolate mixture. Pour into 8 petits pots and chill until ready to serve.

In the living room, float a little additional Grand Marnier on top of each petit pot just before serving.

CHOCOLATE MACAROONS 98

A gem of a cookie, its rich, glossy appearance and ease of preparation make it the perfect accessory for ZABAGLIONE, SUMMER LEMON SOUFFLÉ, PINEAPPLE ICE . . . or whenever you wish that "little something extra".

*Yield
5 dozen*

*Preparation
15 minutes*

*Baking
10 minutes*

    2 ounces unsweetened chocolate
    1 14-ounce can sweetened condensed milk
    2 cups finely shredded coconut
    1 cup chopped nuts
    1 tablespoon strongly brewed coffee
    1 teaspoon almond extract
    ⅛ teaspoon salt

Preheat oven to 350°. In a large, heavy saucepan, combine the chocolate and milk and cook over medium heat, stirring briskly with a whisk until thick and glossy. Remove from heat and add remaining ingredients, stirring with a wooden spoon to blend.

Drop the chocolate mixture by small teaspoonfuls on a greased baking sheet, about an inch apart. Bake 10 minutes or until the bottoms are set. Do not overbake. The macaroons should have a soft, chewy texture. Transfer to waxed paper to cool.

99 CHOCOLATE CAKE with COFFEE FROSTING

Serves 12

Preparation 30 minutes

Every baking enthusiast has a chocolate cake recipe that he or she considers the best. Some truly outstanding ones were submitted for this book and, for a time, it seemed impossible to choose *the one*. After much testing, this recipe took first place as the richest and most appealing to true chocolate lovers. Beware!

> 5 ounces unsweetened chocolate
> ½ cup buttermilk
> 1 cup sugar
> 1 egg, separated
> ½ cup butter, softened
> 1 cup light-brown sugar
> 2 eggs, separated
> 2 cups sifted cake flour
> 1 teaspoon baking soda
> ½ teaspoon salt
> ¾ cup buttermilk
> 1 teaspoon vanilla

Preheat oven to 350°. Butter 2 9-inch cake pans.

In a sauce pan, slowly melt chocolate and add ½ cup buttermilk. With a whisk, stir over low heat until mixture is smooth. Add 1 cup sugar and 1 egg yolk. Stir constantly for 3 minutes or until the custard is thick and smooth. Cool.

Cream butter and brown sugar well. Add 2 egg yolks, one at a time. Resift cake flour with baking soda and salt. Add to butter mixture in 3 parts, alternating with ¾ cup buttermilk. Stir the cooled custard and vanilla into the batter.

Beat 3 egg whites until they are stiff but not dry. Fold into batter. Pour into prepared pans.

Bake for 25–30 minutes or until cake just begins to leave the side of the pans or centers spring to touch. Completely cool in pans before removing. When cool, spread COFFEE FROSTING between layers as well as on top and sides of cake.

> 1 cup butter, softened
> 1/4 teaspoon salt
> 2–3 tablespoons instant coffee, dissolved in
>   1/4 cup hot water
> 3 cups confectioners' sugar
> 2 teaspoons rum or brandy

Combine all ingredients and beat until smooth.

FUDGE SAUCE 100

Heavenly!

Yield
2 cups

Preparation
5 minutes

> 3 squares unsweetened chocolate
> 1/4 cup butter
> 1 cup confectioners' sugar
> 6 tablespoons heavy cream
> 1 teaspoon vanilla
> 1–2 tablespoons Grand Marnier (optional)

In a sauce pan, over low heat, melt chocolate and butter, stirring constantly with a whisk.

When melted, beat in sugar. Add 3 tablespoons cream and continue beating with whisk. When well-blended, beat in remaining cream. Add vanilla and Grand Marnier.

This keeps nicely and makes a popular gift.

101 FROZEN CHOCOLATE TORTE

Serves
8 to 10

Preparation
20 minutes

Baking
90 minutes

Freeze
6 hours

Known to us as "Inge-Lise's Dessert", this heavenly confection was created by a member of our committee who honors her Danish heritage by being a superb cook.

3 egg whites
½ teaspoon cream of tartar
¾ cup sugar
¾ cup chopped pecans
2 cups heavy cream
¾ cup chocolate syrup or sauce
1 teaspoon vanilla
Chocolate shavings
Pecan halves

Preheat oven to 275°.

Beat egg whites until frothy. Add cream of tartar and beat until soft peaks form. Add sugar, 1 tablespoon at a time, and continue beating until very stiff peaks form. Fold in pecans.

Cover 2 baking sheets with brown paper. Using an 8-inch plate, draw a circle on each paper. Divide and spread meringue over each circle, shaping into flat shells.

Bake for 45 minutes. Without opening oven door, turn oven off and do not remove meringues for another 45 minutes. Remove and cool.

When ready to assemble, beat cream until very stiff. Fold in syrup and vanilla.

Spread 1 meringue layer with half of the chocolate cream. Add second meringue and cover top with remaining cream mixture. With a fork, make designs such as a pinwheel on the top. Decorate with chocolate shavings and pecan halves. Freeze at least 6 hours.

Remove from freezer 5–10 minutes before serving.

WALNUT CAKE with CHOCOLATE CREAM 102

This is an unusual, glamorous cake. It is very light in texture, filled with a rich chocolate cream. It should be made a day before serving.

Serves
10 to 12

Preparation
20 minutes

Baking
30 minutes

Chill
2 hours

> 9–10 ounces English walnuts
> 6 eggs, separated
> 1 cup sugar

Preheat oven to 350°. Butter and flour 2 9-inch cake pans. Pulverize the walnuts in a food processor or blender until they become a fine powder. They should yield 2 cups. In a large bowl, beat the egg whites until stiff. In a separate bowl, beat the egg yolks until lemon-colored and fluffy. Gradually beat the sugar into the egg yolks and fold into the egg whites. Fold in the powdered walnuts.

Pour the batter into prepared cake pans and bake 25–30 minutes, or until the cake pulls away from the sides and is lightly browned. *Immediately* invert the pans on racks. Cool slightly then remove cakes from pans and let stand 2–4 hours.

While the cakes cool, prepare the CHOCOLATE CREAM which should be chilled up to 2 hours but no more.

> 3 ounces unsweetened chocolate
> 5 tablespoons sugar
> 1 ½ cups heavy cream

Over medium heat, melt the chocolate in a medium-sized saucepan. With a whisk, stir in the sugar and then the cream. Stir constantly until the mixture *almost* comes to a boil. Immediately remove from heat. Chill as instructed.

When ready to frost the cake, beat the chocolate mixture with an electric beater until it becomes the consistency of whipped cream. Spread between cake layers and then on top and sides of cake. If you wish, sprinkle the top with shaved chocolate for decoration. Refrigerate overnight.

103 WALNUT PIE

Serves
8 to 10

Preparation
10 minutes

Baking
50 minutes

The English walnut trees of northern California are strong and majestic in character, thousands of them darkly defining the rivers and streams that wend their way through our golden foothills. The Indians propagated the fine-flavored fruit, which has become one of California's most valuable industries. WALNUT PIE is a delicious testimony.

> 3 eggs
> ½ cup firmly packed brown sugar
> 1 cup light corn syrup
> ¼ cup butter, melted
> 1 teaspoon cinnamon
> ¼ teaspoon salt
> 1 teaspoon vanilla
> 1 cup broken English walnuts or walnut halves
> 1 9-inch unbaked pastry shell

Preheat oven to 375°.

In a medium-sized bowl, beat the eggs then blend well with the brown sugar, corn syrup, melted butter, cinnamon, salt, and vanilla, in that order. Stir in the nuts. Pour the mixture into the unbaked pastry shell.

Place the pie on the lowest shelf of the oven and bake 50 minutes, or until the filling jiggles only slightly when the dish is gently shaken.

Cool on a wire rack at least 2 hours before cutting. The pie is at its best made a day ahead but kept unrefrigerated.

Truly luscious!

7 egg yolks
¾ cup superfine sugar
1 cup sweet Marsala wine
½ teaspoon vanilla
Grated peel of a lemon half (no white of the rind)
Pinch of cinnamon
1 cup heavy cream, whipped

Put egg yolks, sugar, and wine in the top of a double boiler. (A copper, round-bottomed container is ideal.) Place over hot, not boiling, water. Beat constantly with a whisk, continually scraping sides and bottom of pan. Beat until the mixture forms soft mounds. Remove from heat and continue beating until it has cooled considerably.

When the custard has cooled to room temperature, beat in the vanilla, lemon peel, and cinnamon. Place the bowl in a larger bowl filled with cracked ice and continue to beat until the fluffy mixture is chilled through.

Whip cream until stiff and fold into ice-cold Zabaglione. Pour into tall glasses and chill until serving time. If you wish, place a PRALINE COOKIE with each serving.

105 CARAMEL MERINGUE

Serves 6

Preparation
30 minutes

Baking
1 hour

This was a treasured recipe for lovely dinner parties of the elegant past. You will not readily find a similar one in other cookbooks. It is beautifully light and delicious, and much simpler to prepare than it seems. It may be made in the morning, remaining on your counter until service time. The sauce, though, should be refrigerated.

MERINGUE

2¼ cups granulated sugar
6 egg whites
½ teaspoon vanilla
Pinch of cream of tartar

SAUCE

1 cup milk
½ cup heavy cream
6 egg yolks
1 teaspoon vanilla

Preheat oven to 275°.

Caramelize 1¼ cups sugar by stirring it in a heavy frying pan over moderate heat, using a wooden spatula. When sugar has melted to a rich, caramel brown, pour into a 9½-inch ring mold and tilt the mold until its sides are well-coated. Do not scrape or wash frying pan, as you will be using it to make your sauce.

With an electric mixer (we do not suggest a portable electric beater), beat the egg whites until they begin to take shape. Gradually add ½ cup sugar and continue beating until the whites are *very* stiff (stiffer than for angel food cake). Beat in vanilla and cream of tartar. Fold in remaining ½ cup sugar.

Pile mixture into the caramel-coated mold, carefully removing any air pockets. Place mold, uncovered, in a larger pan containing ½-inch warm water. Bake one hour or until the meringue is high, firm, and light brown on top. Quickly loosen the edges of the meringue with a knife dipped in cold water to prevent tearing. *Immediately* unmold on your prettiest platter, allowing the caramel liquid to drip over the meringue. Do not be concerned about the hardened caramel that will remain in the mold. Leave it there until scrubbing time when hot water will melt it away.

To prepare the sauce, warm 1 cup milk in the same pan in which the sugar was caramelized. Pour the cream over the egg yolks and beat well. Add to the warm, not hot, milk and stir *briskly* with a flat whisk over low to moderate heat until sauce is as thick as very heavy cream. Do not allow to boil or it will curdle. Immediately remove from heat. Add vanilla. Refrigerate until serving time, then pass in a separate bowl.

You may double this recipe, using a larger mold, but bake the meringue 10–15 minutes longer.

Note: You may not care for the flavor of the sauce by itself, but when combined with the meringue, it becomes heavenly!

106 CRÊPES SUZETTE

Serves 12

Yield
36 crêpes

Preparation
45 minutes

We guarantee that your dinner party will be a smashing success with this fabulous dessert! Beautiful without being flamboyant, you will be delighted with the ease of its presentation.

> 2 whole eggs
> 2 egg yolks
> 1¾ cups milk
> ⅔ cup flour
> 1 tablespoon sugar
> Pinch of salt
> 2 tablespoons butter, melted
> 1 tablespoon cognac

Combine eggs and egg yolks and beat well. Beat in milk. With a whisk, stir this mixture into dry ingredients until batter is smooth. Add melted butter and cognac and let stand 1 hour.

Heat a well-greased, 5-inch skillet or crêpe pan. Pour in enough batter to barely cover bottom, about one tablespoon. Rotate pan quickly to spread batter thinly and evenly. Cook crêpe until light brown. Flip over and cook other side.

Stack the crêpes flat, until all are made, then spread each one with the following mixture:

> ½ cup butter, softened
> ½ cup confectioners' sugar
> Grated rind of 2 oranges
> Juice of 1 orange
> ¼ teaspoon lemon juice
> ¼ cup Curaçao or rum

Cream together the above ingredients. After spreading on crêpes, roll them up or fold in quarters like a handkerchief. At this point, the crêpes may be frozen.

To serve, thaw crêpes and keep warm in following sauce:

>1 cup clover honey
>¼ cup melted butter
>2 tablespoons Curaçao or rum
>½ cup hot brandy

Heat together honey, butter, and Curaçao, and add to crêpes in a chafing dish. To ignite, pour ½ cup hot brandy over the crêpes and light quickly. Magnificent!

PRALINE COOKIES 107

Light and crisp.

Yield
3–4 dozen

>3 tablespoons butter, melted
>1 cup firmly packed dark brown sugar
>1 egg, beaten
>5 tablespoons flour
>1 cup pecan halves
>1 teaspoon vanilla
>Pinch of salt

Preparation
15 minutes

Preheat oven to 350°.

Combine butter and sugar. Mix in remaining ingredients well. Thoroughly grease a cookie sheet and coat with flour. Recoat the cookie sheet before each baking. Drop batter by scant teaspoonfuls, 5 inches apart, including a nut half each time. Bake 8–10 minutes.

After cookies are baked, wait 1 minute, no longer, before removing them with a spatula to a rack to cool. If they stick, briefly rewarm cookie sheet.

Yield
2 loaves

Serves 12

Preparation
20 minutes

Baking
1 hour

Everything about this recipe is a surprise! You'll love it for afternoon teas or morning coffees.

1 cup water
½ cup margarine*
2 cups flour
½ cup margarine
2 tablespoons water
3 eggs
1 teaspoon almond flavoring

In a medium saucepan, bring 1 cup water and ½ cup margarine to a boil. Remove from heat and stir in 1 cup of the flour with a wooden spoon, beating well until smooth. Set aside.

In a medium-sized bowl, combine remaining 1 cup flour and ½ cup margarine, blending well. Add 2 tablespoons water and mix with a wooden spoon until dough tends to form a ball. Divide in half and place on an ungreased cookie sheet. Use your fingers to flatten into two ¼ inch thick strips, each measuring 3 x 12 inches, keeping them an inch apart.

To the mixture in the saucepan, add the 3 eggs, one at a time, beating well after each addition with a wooden spoon until smooth. Add almond extract and mix well. Spread mixture on each dough strip to within ¼-inch of edges. Bake 1 hour at 350° without opening oven. Cool 10 minutes, then frost.

¼ cup butter, softened
1 cup confectioners' sugar
1 tablespoon milk
½ teaspoon almond extract
¼–½ cup sliced almonds, toasted

Combine the butter, sugar, milk, and almond extract, and spread over warm pastries. Sprinkle with nuts.

Note: In this recipe, margarine is preferred to butter.

Crescents of almond-filled pastry, these cookies are scrumptious at a tea, for Christmas, or high-lighting any lovely occasion. They are far less complicated to make than the recipe appears.

Yield
4 dozen

Preparation
1 hour

Chill
1 hour

Baking
12 minutes

2¼ cups sifted flour
½ teaspoon salt
1 cup butter, softened
4 tablespoons ice water
8 ounces almond paste
1 egg
2 tablespoons granulated sugar
⅓ cup ground blanched almonds
⅔ cup confectioners' sugar

Combine flour and salt in a medium-sized bowl. Cut in butter with a pastry blender until the mixture is crumbly. Add ice water, 1 tablespoon at a time, mixing well with a fork. Divide and shape the pastry into 3 equal rounds. Wrap each in plastic film and chill at least 1 hour.

In a small bowl, break up almond paste with a fork. Beat in egg, granulated sugar, and ground almonds. The mixture will be sticky. Turn out onto a lightly floured surface. Shape into a ball with floured hands and divide into thirds. Shape each third into a rope measuring ½-inch in diameter and 16 inches long. Cut each rope into 16 1-inch pieces. Reserve.

When the pastry is chilled, roll out one round at a time to ⅛-inch thickness on a lightly floured board. The pastry should measure 12 inches square. Trim the rough edges. Using a ruler and a sharp knife or pastry wheel, cut the pastry into 16 3-inch squares.

Place 1 piece of almond mixture diagonally across each pastry square. Lift a corner over filling and roll. Pinch the ends to enclose. Curve the pastry into a crescent. Place 1 inch apart on ungreased cookie sheet. Bake at 400° for 12 minutes until edges just begin to brown. Coat the warm cookies with confectioners' sugar.

110 PECAN TASSIES

Yield
48 tarts

Preparation
45 minutes

Baking
40 minutes

It is told that this recipe was a closely guarded secret for many, many years. After sampling it, we could understand why. The tarts are perfection.

1 cup butter, softened
6 ounces cream cheese, softened
2 cups flour
½ cup butter, softened
1 cup sugar
1 egg, lightly beaten
1½ cups chopped pecans
1 cup chopped dates
1 tablespoon vanilla

Preheat oven to 350°.

In a large bowl, combine the 1 cup butter, cream cheese, and flour. Mix until well-blended. Divide the dough into 4 equal parts, then separate each part into 12 balls, all the same size. Place the balls in the 2-inch sections of 4 ungreased, miniature muffin tins. Using your thumb and forefinger, press each ball into its cup, working the dough evenly up the sides to the rim.

Cream the remaining ½ cup butter with the sugar. Add the rest of the ingredients and mix well. Divide among the unbaked shells, filling each completely.

Bake until golden brown, about 30–40 minutes. Cool on racks before removing the tarts from their tins. When serving, sprinkle with powdered sugar.

Not only are these tarts lovely for a tea table, but they are a wonderfully easy dessert for large parties. They will keep several days before serving or may be frozen.

CONTRIBUTORS

League Members

Ann Mitchell Shuey Baker
Virginia Jameson Bechtold
Suzanne Lafferty Beim
Margaret Rossotti Beltramo
Ginger McCauley Beman
Betty Leonard Breyman
Carolyn Fulgham Butcher
Bunny Rankin Davis
Ann Goodwin Ditz
Letitia Doud Ferrari
Betsy Grube Gifford
Ginger Alfs Glockner
Joan Emery Hagey
Kingsley Fitzhugh Jack
Jean Cook Jacobs
Cindy Monroe Kirk
Kristin Ekstrom Klint
Ann Wahlund Latta
Mary Liz Hufnagel Maletis
Lynn Hochschwender McGowin
Bonnie Stewart Mickelson
Nancy Sothern Mueller
Margaret Freed New
Virginia Rockwell Nile

Nancy Smith Norvell
Anne Draper Brown Page
Inge-Lise Nielsen Parker
Judith Gillfillan Pence
Joanna Fagergren Pistenmaa
Betsy Rabbitt Pomeroy
Marlyn Moore Pratt
Carolyn Wiedemann Reller
Ann Haney Rice
Pamela Flebbe Roach
Karen Strandhagen Ross
Diana Hunter Roth
Pat Dale Sheehan
Sonia Wakefield Shepard
Karen Garling Sickel
Jamie Bingham Sidells
Virginia Michael Sproul
Shirley Cooter Stewart
Christine Larson Terborgh
Cynthia Nathan Toussaint
Dianne Gillette Violich
Marva Mullins Warnock
Nancy Swartz Wilson
Catharine Howell Zander

League Friends

Susan Schiffman Bass
Judy Nelligan Blommer
Diana Dexter Bryan
Lois McCubbin Burrows
Dorothy Bjorklund Cartan
Janice Rottle Conomos
Joanne Rohwedder Evans

Virginia Burnham Farewell
Marcia Oslund Guzy
Ellen Drucker Krinsky
Peggy Fitzgerald Nute
Lou Seibert Pappas
Mimi Creighton Paris
Maureen Kostelecky Smith

Dalva Galeno Youngblood

The purpose of the Junior League is exclusively educational and charitable and is to promote voluntarism, to develop the potential of its members for voluntary participation in community affairs, and to demonstrate the effectiveness of the volunteer.

THE ARTIST

Linda Newberry's remarkably sensitive drawings are of plants and creatures that one may encounter on walks through the grasslands and marshes, riparian and woodland areas of northern California. A native Californian, she is the resident naturalist and teacher at Deer Hollow Farm on the San Antonio Open Space Preserve in Los Altos, California. Through her art, she demonstrates to her students the intricate reality and sensitivity of the natural world. She has designed and illustrated many of the brochures used by environmental education organizations on the San Francisco Peninsula. She worked closely with our 1973–1976 JUNIOR LEAGUE *project,* Environmental Volunteers, *a program that trained and equipped volunteers for classroom and field teaching.*

Among the pages of this book, you will find in plant life the mariposa lily, fiddleneck fern, baby blue-eyes, lupine, amole (soaproot), zigadene (star lily), bed straw, miners lettuce, sedges, redwood sorrel, wild columbine, Douglas iris, trillium, wild ginger, horsetail, California poppy, shooting stars, leopard lily, and brass buttons. Inhabiting this world are silvery blues (butterflies), a dusky-footed woodrat, Merriam chipmunk, brush rabbit, harvest mouse, tree squirrel, tree frog, English sparrow, red-wing blackbird, hermit thrush, Virginia rail, and a pair of ruddy ducks.

THE DESIGNER

Gerald W. Stratford is a fourth-generation Californian whose family has contributed to the Bay Area tradition of fine typography, printing and book binding since 1906. The Stratford Colophon symbolically recalls the phoenix to commemorate the growth of this tradition from the ashes of San Francisco's great fire. Mr. Stratford has designed books for the California Palace of the Legion of Honor and the De Young Museum and his typographic work has been repeatedly chosen for awards, most recently in the 21st annual exhibit of the Type Directors Club of New York.

THE TYPE

The original punches of the type cut by John Baskerville of Birmingham are still in existence. They were sold by Baskerville's widow to Beaumarchais and have descended through various French foundries to Deberny & Peignot and are now at the Cambridge University Press. Baskerville is a round letter and while maintaining some of the feeling of old-style forms is rightly classified as the first of the transitional romans in England. There is more differentiation of thick and thin strokes than in Caslon, the serifs on the lower case letters are more nearly horizontal and the stress nearer the vertical. The monotype version used here has an italic much regularized from the Deberny & Peignot original. This book was elegantly set with great care and love by the journeymen of the Mackenzie-Harris chapel in San Francisco.